Western Frontiersmen Series, XXIII

Dr. Jacob Davis Babcock Stillman
He visited Texas for six months in 1855 before settling in California. This
photograph was made at some later date.

Wanderings
in the
Southwest in 1855

by
J. D. B. Stillman

Edited with an Introduction
by
Ron Tyler

THE ARTHUR H. CLARK COMPANY
Spokane, Washington ❧ 1990

———

LIBRARY OF CONGRESS CATALOG CARD NUMBER 88-71687
ISBN 0-87062-192-0

Library of Congress Cataloging-in-Publication Data

Stillman, J.D.B. (Jacob Davis Babcock), 1819-1888.
    Wanderings in the Southwest in 1855 / by J.D.B. Stillman ; edited with an
introduction by Ron Tyler.
    194 pp.   cm. — (Western frontiersmen series ; 23)
    Includes bibliographical references.
    ISBN 0-87062-192-0
    1. Texas—Description and travel.   2. Stillman, J.D.B. (Jacob Davis Babcock),
1819-1888—Journeys—Texas.   I. Tyler, Ronnie C., 1941-   II. Title.
III. Series.
F391.S86   1989
917.6404'5—dc20   88-71687
                                                                         CIP

Contents

Illustrations

Acknowledgments

I am indebted to many people in the preparation of this book, including William Howze, Director of Special Projects at the Amon Carter Museum, and Paula Tyler, my wife, who read the introduction and offered constructive suggestions for its improvement. Librarians in both Texas and California provided kind assistance, but most helpful was Margaret Stoner McLean, former newspaper archivist at the Amon Carter Museum, who not only read the manuscript, but offered suggestions as to others who might be able to help with various portions of it. Milan Hughston, Assistant Librarian at the Amon Carter Museum, promptly ordered materials on inter-library loan, and Ben Huseman, Research Assistant at the Carter Museum, shared his research into the German newspapers in Texas. Various key elements of research would have gone wanting had it not been for his expertise in the German language and diligence in research.

Introduction

Texas was still a frontier state in 1855, hardly removed from the era of "dry beef, black coffee, sweet potatoes, and other hard features" of a previous decade that had prompted a Tyler County settler to declare it the "most perfect purgatory of any place on earth." It still reeled from the effects of the financial crash of 1837 that had sent dozens of Eastern land speculators and bankers into a panic. Thousands of small farmers seeking refuge from bankruptcy arrived, increasing agricultural production and imbuing the state with a physical vigor that few others could match. Senator Sam Houston, the hero of the battle of San Jacinto, first president of the Republic, and now a national political figure, defended slavery against the moral and expansionist charges of William Lloyd Garrison in a Boston debate that year, and the state's first historian, Huntsville lawyer Henderson Yoakum, began his monumental work with the assertion that "there is no country of like extent."[1]

This was the Texas that thirty-six year old Jacob Davis Babcock Stillman, an adventurous New York physician, chose to visit in 1855. The state had been thoroughly explored by the various government and private surveys, but the settlement line had hardly extended beyond the 100th meridian and vast wil-

---

[1] Quoted in William Ransom Hogan, *The Texas Republic: A Social and Economic History* (Austin: Univ. of Tex. Press, 1969 reprint), p. 34; See Barnes F. Lathrop, *Migration Into East Texas, 1835-1860: A Study from the United States Census* (Austin: Tex. State Hist. Assn., 1949); Llerena B. Friend, *Sam Houston: The Great Designer* (Austin: Univ. of Tex. Press, 1954), pp. 236-37; and Henderson Yoakum, *History of Texas, From Its First Settlement in 1685 to Its Annexation to the United States in 1846*, 2 vols. (New York: Redfield, 1856), I, p. 6.

dernesses still existed. A line of forts, from Belknap and Phantom Hill on the north to Clark on the Rio Grande, shielded the frontier from Indian raids, while Fort Lancaster and Fort Davis had been established to keep the road from San Antonio to El Paso open. Galveston, on the coast, and San Antonio, in the hinterland, became the state's two largest cities as the western fringes of settlement pushed past the European settlements of Castroville and Fredericksburg west and north of San Antonio.[2]

Stillman had heard all of his life that Texas was an "Elysium of rogues." "Gone to Texas"—or "G.T.T."—was a common expression and, scrawled across a door usually meant that the occupant had departed his homestead, either bankrupt or a fugitive from justice, for the wilds of the Texas frontier. Some of the "rogues" might still have roamed the countryside in 1855, but fertile lands and natural beauty had overcome thousands of would-be immigrants' fears, and the state was growing rapidly. An 1848 census registered 158,356 people. That number had grown to 271,150 by the time the 1850 census was completed, and the 1860 census would count another almost 400,000 inhabitants. "It has been the fate of Texas to attract the attention of the world to a greater extent than was ever done by the same number of the human family in any age," a writer for the Matagorda newspaper had claimed in 1844.[3]

A distinguished looking, talented man who seemed equally at home in New York social and intellectual circles as on the Western frontier, Stillman had considerable travel experience

[2] Information of the surveys of Texas can be found in William H. Goetzmann, *Army Exploration in the American West, 1803-1863* (New Haven: Yale Univ. Press, 1959), particularly in the chapters on the Boundary Survey and the Pacific Railroad Surveys. The map on page 44 of D. W. Meinig's *Imperial Texas: An Interpretive Essay in Cultural Geography* (Austin: Univ. of Tex. Press, 1969) illustrates the settlement patterns before the Civil War.

[3] Quoted in Mark E. Nackman, *A Nation Within a Nation: The Rise of Texas Nationalism* (Port Washington, N. Y: Kennikat Press, 1975), pp. 9-12, quote on pp. 11-12.

before arriving in Texas. Born in Schenectady, New York, in 1819, he was educated at Union College, with an M.D. degree following from New York City's College of Physicians and Surgeons. After practicing at Bellevue Hospital, Stillman had moved to California and had established himself in Sacramento shortly before his thirtieth birthday.

His journey around the Horn to San Francisco had been his first adventure. In a highly unusual action, the passengers wrested control of the vessel from the dictatorial captain at Rio de Janeiro, and Stillman and his friends had sailed into San Francisco on August 5, 1849. While most of his fellow passengers had proceeded immediately to the gold fields, Stillman and Dr. John F. Morse had settled in Sacramento, where they established the city's first hospital. They were receiving patients by January 9, 1850, when the now-famous flood hit the city. Stillman worked for two full days and nights treating patients and fearing all the while that the building would collapse under the pounding of the wind and waves. Soon after the flood, a fever and jaundice complicated by severe homesickness ended his California sojourn and by the end of 1850 he was back in practice in New York City. His marriage and subsequent tour of the Continent in 1854 had renewed his wanderlust, so by 1855 he was intrigued by the notion of following in the steps of his friend an acquaintance Frederick Law Olmsted, who had just returned from a well-publicized, five-month trip to Texas.[4]

---

[4] The biographical material on Stillman comes from his *Around the Horn to California in 1849*, foreword by Kenneth M. Johnson (Palo Alto, Calif: Lewis Osborne, 1967), pp. 5-8. Stillman published extensively in *The Overland Monthly* from 1868 until 1875. Browne's recollections of the journey are recorded in David Michael Goodman, *A Western Panorama, 1849-1875: The Travels, Writings and Influence of J. Ross Browne* (Glendale: Arthur H. Clark Co., 1966), pp. 31-32. Stillman also was responsible for founding one of the first medical societies in California, the Medico-Chirurgical Association, and was elected recording secretary. See Jacob D. B. Stillman, *The Gold Rush Letters of J. D. B. Stillman*, Intro. by Kenneth

Stillman wanted to study Texas's "resources and natural history," but it is evident from his letters that he anticipated a beauty that the word-shy pioneers could not have described even if they had understood. The young doctor was a full-fledged member of a generation that had fallen completely in love with America's natural beauty. With representatives among the artists, philosophers, theologians, historians, and other intellectuals, these young nationalists possessed a deep reverence for nature that found its expression in paintings of the Hudson River School, writings by Ralph Waldo Emerson and Henry David Thoreau, and periodicals such as *The Crayon,* a short-lived but leading journal of landscape art published in New York City that would be the vehicle by which Stillman related his Texas adventure.

Sailing from New Orleans, Stillman entered what is today Matagorda Bay on the Gulf of Mexico and landed at Indianola in May 1855. Indianola had been founded as Carlshafen by Prince Carl of Solms-Braunfels in 1844 as the port of entry for the thousands of German immigrants the Adelsverein was preparing to bring to Texas. In 1849 Charles Morgan, of the Harris & Morgan Line, moved his company's docks from Port Lavaca to a site three miles below Indianola on Powder Horn Bayou. This is probably where Stillman landed, and unimpressed with

---

Johnson (Palo Alto, Calif: Lewis Osborne, 1967), pp. 7-10; George D. Lyman, "The Scalpel Under Three Flags in California," *Calif. Hist. Soc. Quar.,* IV (June 1925), pp. 189-90. See also Jacob D. B. Stillman, *An 1850 Voyage: San Francisco to Baltimore by Sea and by Land,* Intro. by John Barr Tompkins (Palo Alto, Calif: Lewis Osborne, 1976), pp. 5-9; Charles Capen McLaughlin and Charles E. Beveridge (eds.), *The Papers of Frederick Law Olmsted: The Formative Years, 1822 to 1852,* 2 vols. (Baltimore and London: Johns Hopkins Univ. Press, 1977-1981), I, pp. 13-15. Olmsted's *A Journey Through Texas; or, A Saddle-Trip on the Southwestern Frontier: With a Statistical Appendix* (N.Y: Dix, Edwards & Co., 1857) has been reprinted four times: first by James Howard, who abridged it (Austin: Von Boeckmann-Jones Press, 1962), then in facsimile by Burt Franklin (1969), the Univ. of Tex. Press (1978), and Time-Life Books (1981). See John H. Jenkins, *Basic Texas Books: An Annotated Bibliography of Selected Works for a Research Library* (Austin: Jenkins Publishing Co., 1983), pp. 420-421.

the "illimitable expanse of water and prairie" and feeling that he had absorbed the "sum total" of the village in a moment, he reboarded the yacht on which he had come and rode the spring tide further up the southwest side of Lavaca Bay to Port Lavaca. "Another pier . . . another collection of pine board houses," Stillman wrote, but he gamely set out to follow in the footsteps of thousands of newly-arrived German immigrants who had ventured into the region before him.[5]

This was the land that had attracted dozens of *empresarios* and thousands of immigrants since the 1820s, that had become a *cause célèbre* in the slavery controversy of the 1830s, and that had sparked the war with Mexico in 1846. It was a country still plagued by Comanche raiders who usually were after horses but who all too often took lives as well. It was an undeniably rough place, and its citizens were proud of it. "If you have not got the stamina of a real man in you, do not come," warned an Austin resident. "If you do, you will fret, and whine, and whimper, and sneak back to the old States, disgusted at our roughness and newness."[6] But it was also a state with an undeniable spirit and an almost irresistible appeal for those who, like Stillman, searched for spots where the rough edge of civilization met the "untrodden wilds" of the frontier, where he might satisfy his "curiosity" and "enjoy and commune with Nature."

At Port Lavaca Stillman purchased a horse and set out alone on May 4 for San Antonio by way of Anaqua, Goliad, and Helena. He traveled much of the route that Olmsted had covered—along the coastline, San Antonio, then the historical

---

[5] All of Stillman's quotes come from the "Wanderings in the Southwest," which are reproduced below in their entirety. For information on the history of Indianola, see Rudolph Leopold Biesele, *The History of the German Settlements in Texas, 1831-1861,* (Austin: Press of Von Boeckmann-Jones Co., 1930), p. 112; Brownson Malsch, *Indianola: The Mother of Western Texas* (Austin: Shoal Creek Pubrs., Inc., 1977), pp. 5-13, 39-43.

[6] *The Texas Republican* (Marshall), Mar. 19, 1853; Mar. 25, Aug. 5, 1854.

and cultural center of the state, and the German settlements north of the city—and visited some of the same people. Both were much impressed with the Germans, for Stillman, like Olmsted, shared many of their cultural values, including a horror of slavery. Stillman spent many hours recalling the charming Rhine villages that he and his wife had visited the previous year and felt that these civilized immigrants were a marked and pleasant contrast to the abrasive and unlettered Texans he had met. He tarried in San Antonio in the company of Adolph Douai, the editor of the *San Antonio Zeitung,* and even opened a practice to help maintain himself while in the city.[7]

When Olmsted had left San Antonio he had gone to Mexico. He had returned east by way of the Gulf coast, failing to see West Texas. Because Stillman could not find a companion for the trip to Mexico and dared not attempt it alone, he again relied upon his medical expertise to win him a place with the army as he traveled west to Fort Clark, Camp Lancaster, and other points along the newly-opened road from San Antonio to El Paso as far west as the Pecos River. He penetrated unsettled areas, risking an Indian attack to see first-hand the "wilds" of Texas. In a wilderness flash flood he lost the sketchbook in which he, like many of his contemporaries, recorded his hurried impressions.[8]

Rough rides over long and muddy roads did not deter his romantic spirit, nor did periodic residences in poorly-constructed log houses, permeated with the stench of a frontier more con-

---

[7] See Stillman's advertisement in the *San Antonio Zeitung,* July 21, 1855, p. 2, col. 6. Stillman offered his medical services to the citizens from his office over J. M. Devine's drug store on the plaza. The ad also appeared July 28 and August 4.

[8] Douai published a letter from Stillman regarding the Indian skirmish in the *San Antonio Zeitung,* Nov. 3, 1855, p. 2, col. 5, noting that Stillman was serving as doctor at Fort Lancaster. *The Galveston Weekly News,* Nov. 13, 1855, p. 1, col. 9, picked up the story from a letter written from Camp Lancaster to the *San Antonio Herald.*

cerned with shelter than with cleanliness. He learned that, while the Indian threat was real, lack of life's necessities such as sugar, flour, and coffee aggravated the daily struggle for survival more meaningfully than did the war-painted natives. Completion of the modest Governor's Mansion in Austin symbolically ameliorated the frontier crudeness, but Stillman probably would have readily agreed with a well-known saying attributed to Noah Smithwick, one of Austin's original colonists, but probably repeated by many Texans: early Texas was "heaven for men and dogs," but "hell for women and oxen."

Stillman left Texas in November, concluding a six-month tour. Meanwhile, his letters had begun appearing in *The Crayon* in June, virtually as soon as the editor received them, and ran through April 1856. Soon after his return from Texas, Stillman once again moved to California. He settled in Sacramento in 1856 and resumed his practice, but yet another flood, in 1861-1862, sent him scurrying to the higher ground of San Francisco. There he continued to practice, serving as coroner for both the city and county. He was elected to the Board of Education and served as a trustee for the Lick School of Trades, but turned down a position on the medical staff of the new University of California.[9]

Stillman wrote quite a bit about his travels. In addition to his Texas letters, he published essays in *The Overland Monthly* and wrote his memoirs in 1877, *Seeking the Golden Fleece; a Record of Pioneer Life in California.*[10]

He also became involved in the famous and spirited dispute between Leland Stanford, Jr. and Frederick MacCrellish, publisher of the San Francisco *Alta California*. Stanford contended that a running horse could have all four hooves off the ground

---

[9] Stillman, *Around the Horn,* pp. 8-9.

[10] Jacob D. B. Stillman, *Seeking the Golden Fleece; a Record of Pioneer Life in California* . . . (San Francisco and N. Y: A. Roman & Co., 1877).

simultaneously, and MacCrellish took the other point of view in this aged quarrel. It surely would have ended there had not technology developed to the point that it was possible to resolve the argument. Stanford employed Stillman and photograper Eadweard J. Muybridge, who had only recently perfected the instantaneous shutter, to investigate. Some claimed that Stanford and MacCrellish also wagered $50,000 on the outcome.

Muybridge made a series of stop-action photographs on the Stanford stock farm at Palo Alto, and Stillman studied the anatomy and physiology of the horse. The result was a book entitled *The Horse in Motion,* written by Stillman and illustrated by reproduction of Muybridge's photographs, which clearly proved that Stanford was right. Stillman's name was prominently displayed on the title page as author, but Muybridge received no credit for his photographs, and, having taken the precaution of copyrighting the images, he sued Stanford. Stanford won the suit, but the book sold poorly and was finally "thrown on the market for what it would bring."[11]

In 1880 Stillman turned his attention to plants, particularly dates and grapes, as he revived the interest in wines that he had acquired during his European travels. He auctioned his vast library through Edward S. Spear and Company and bought a farm near Redlands, in San Bernardino County. He imported vines from France and Italy and contributed significantly to the development of the California wine industry. Toward the end of his life he considered himself primarily a viticulturist. Dr. Stillman died March 1, 1888, at his country home in Lugo-

---

11 Stillman, *Around the Horn,* pp. 8-9; Robert Bartlett Haas, *Eadweard Muybridge: The Stanford Years, 1872-1882* (Palo Alto, Calif: Stanford Univ. Art Museum, 1972), p. 27; quoted in Haas, *Muybridge: Man in Motion* (Berkeley: Univ. of California, 1976), p. 142n. The book in question is Jacob D. B. Stillman, *The Horse in Motion as Shown by Instantaneous Photography with a Study on Animal Mechanics. Founded on Anatomy and the Revelations of the Camera, in Which is Demonstrated the Theory of Quadrupedal Locomotion* (Boston: J. R. Osgood and Co., 1882).

nia, San Bernardino County, California. He left a widow, his second wife, four sons, and two daughters.[12]

His "Wanderings in the Southwest" were written entirely during and about his six months in Texas in 1855, a crucial, complex, and little understood time in the state's history. Texas had developed for centuries as a Spanish, then as a Mexican province. After a few years of occupation, Anglo-Americans wrenched it from the grasp of Mexico and thrust it into nationhood in less than four months. Following ten uncertain years as an independent nation, it had become a state, a central figure in one of the greatest expansionist triumphs in American history. Many Texans did not understand the opposition that had always existed to slavery and its growth, and it is, therefore, no surprise that they might not have comprehended the subtleties of American politics. Couple these problems with the complexities introduced by the large-scale migration into the state that followed admission into the Union and the crucial nature of these years can be better understood. They probably would be better studied today but for the Civil War, which so quickly rendered these questions moot. We can renew them in retrospect and be grateful for a source as fresh as Stillman's letters.

The Crayon was the ideal format for Stillman's letters. It frequently published essays by the leading American landscape artists such as Asher B. Durand and assumed leadership among artistic intelligentsia. "Untamed nature everywhere asserts her claim upon us," wrote the editor in 1855, "and the recognition of this claim constitutes an essential part of our Art."[13] Stillman felt that he had found a vestage of that nature in Texas. "No-

---

[12] Stillman, *Around the Horn*, pp. 8-9. For a catalogue of Stillman's library, see Jacob D. B. Stillman, *Catalogue of Books to be Sold at Auction on Friday, September 24, 1880, Being the Medical and Miscellaneous Library of Dr. J. D. B. Stillman, Comprising Many Rare and Valuable English Books . . .* ([San Francisco]: Alta California Printing House, [1880]). See also *Daily Alta California* (San Francisco), Mar. 5, 1888.

[13] *The Crayon*, Apr. 11, 1855.

where have I seen nature display so much of the chastened beauty, or rugged grandeur . . .; nowhere have I seen realized, in so high a degree, the charms of the classical *Arcadia* as in the rolling grassy regions of West Texas." "For purposes of settlement or pursuit of health, or enjoyment of nature in her 'visible forms' and primitive loveliness," he wrote, Texas was perfect.

Stillman's letters in *The Crayon* received limited circulation, and his observations remain virtually unknown today, even to historians who have searched for nineteenth-century travel accounts of Texas and the South.[14] They were known to Olmsted, who included them in his bibliography, but through this publication, they will now be known to a much broader audience.

Except for an occasional repeated word, which I have omitted (and indicated with an ellipsis), I have transcribed these essays exactly as they appear on the microfilm copy of *The Crayon,* which is in the library of the Amon Carter Museum and which was made from the original eight-volume set in the collection of the New York Public Library.

RON TYLER

---

[14] The Stillman letters are not listed in Marilyn McAdams Sibley, *Travelers in Texas, 1761-1860* (Austin: Univ. of Tex. Press, 1967), or Ellis M. Coulter, *Travels in the Confederate States, a Bibliography* (Norman: Univ. of Okla. Press, 1948). "Wanderings in the Southwest" is listed in C. W. Raines, *A Bibliography of Texas: Being a Descriptive List of Books, Pamphlets, and Documents Relating to Texas in Print and Manuscript Since 1536* . . . (Austin: The Gammel Book Co., 1896), p. 196, but Raines does not indicate that it is a series of letters or that they are published in *The Crayon.*

The Crayon (New York), I (June 27, 1855), pp. 404-05.

Wanderings in the Southwest
No. 1

Texas, May 18th.

A few days since, I left the New Orleans steamer at the terminus of her route, and deposited myself, with my baggage, in
a . . . yacht for Indianola.[1] Arriving there, I found a long pier
running out into the shoal, milky water, and thereon sitting a
few men and boys fishing, but apparently with little success. I
walked up into the town—a few frame houses prematurely
old, two or three stores, a tavern-stand deserted, a mule with
saddle on, and head hanging low and drowsily, half-a-dozen
idle men, sitting on boxes—and the whole surrounded by an
illimitable expanse of water and prairie, was the sum total of
Indianola. I returned to the yacht, and had my baggage put on
board again to go to Port Lavacca [*sic*].[2] A gentle southern
breeze wafted us slowly along thitherwards. A long file of
pelicans, apparently encumbered by the weight of their enormous bills, were slowly flapping their silent way from their
hunting-grounds near the sea-shore, and numerous blackhead-
ed gulls followed us with a shrill cry for small favors from
the galley. The shore everywhere presents a bank twelve or
fifteen feet high, abrupt, from the constant invasion of the

---

[1] Formerly the port through which the military posts in Texas were supplied,
Indianola, on the west shore of Matagorda Bay, was crushed by devastating hurricanes
in 1875 and 1886. Originally named Powderhorn and later called Karlshaven by
German immigrants, the city was one of the main ports of entry in Texas when Stillman visited it in 1855. Walter P. Webb, H. Bailey Carroll, and Eldon Stephen Branda
(eds.), *The Handbook of Texas,* 3 vols. (Austin: Tex. State Hist. Assn., 1952, 1976),
I, p. 883.

[2] Located in Calhoun County on a bluff overlooking Lavaca Bay, Port Lavaca was
founded in 1840. It was made the county seat after a hurricane destroyed Indianola
in 1886. *Ibid.,* II, p. 395.

waves. The water is shoal, leaving, when the tide is out, light-colored mud flats.

Another pier, built on piles, with several schooners loading with cotton, another collection of pine board houses; many clumsy, broad-wheeled, covered carts, with a small drove of cattle before each of them—we are at Port Lavacca. I decided to send my baggage by one of the Mexican carts, and to purchase a horse, and travel at my leisure out of the beaten road. My object being to enjoy and commune with Nature, I shall travel alone, that even the sound of another's voice may not disturb the harmony. I went to a stable to get a horse. There was one which was very highly recommended to me. It was the property of a Mexican, and was of a light dun color. Age and hard service protruded with each particular bone—his forefeet spread apart, while his knees nearly rubbed each other—the hoofs were flat and much split. I am but a poor judge of horse-flesh, but I was not favorably impressed with the first sight of this Buono [Bueno?] Caballo, but this was of Spanish stock, and there was no knowing what he might do, so I requested the owner to mount and show him up. He walked, he trotted, and, animated by the zeal of the rider, he did make a faint effort to gallop, but it was a melancholy display of spirit. But, said the owner, the chief quality in a horse was to be a good walker. I could have him for just forty-five dollars, and I must close at once, as the owner would leave town with him in an hour if he was not sold. I went to another stable where I found "a mountain pony," of fine qualities, which could endure any kind of usage, and live on grass exclusively. He was already saddled, and I might have him for forty dollars, saddle included. I had thought that one of the distinguishing qualities of the mountain pony was the high small hoof, similar to the mule's, but this specimen had them more spreading than the first horse, and as badly split. His weight was about that of a Mexican mule, and his chest so narrow that a common dinner-knife could reach through it. His face was covered with incrustations, and, although I did not know what quality the muscle of a mountain pony might have, it appeared to me that the question might be raised by the natives on the road, why I did not "pack" the horse and carry him rather than permit him to carry me. I directed the saddle to be removed, and a red, quivering denudation came to sight. Generous fellow, he would have given me the saddle on the horse's back! But this was nothing at all—in two or three days that would all be well, and he poured from a bottle some unetuous matter which was to heal it up at once. This was the end of a day spent among the horse-jockeys in Texas, who, I venture to say, will sustain the reputation of the fraternity in any part of the world.

I next applied to one of the old Texans, whom I have generally found to be a superior class of men. He sent his Mexican vaccaro [vaquero] out to the ranch, where he had a herd of two hundred, to bring some in. He returned the next morning with three, from which I might choose, the prices ranging from forty-five to sixty-five dollars. I made choice of a fine specimen of the native Mexican wild stock, bearing the token of a former possession in a curious hieroglyphic, branded on his left thigh. From his dark brown color, the Mexicans call him "Pelicano," the pelican. His tail reaches quite to the ground, and his mane is long, hanging wildly about his face. His nostrils are wide, as is the space between his eyes, which are so quick in their movements, and yet so kind and confiding, that no sooner had they looked into mine than a mutual attachment sprang up between us, and I resolved to become the proprietor of Pelicano. His life has been spent on the prairie—his little round hoof, smooth as polished horn, had never had its normal proportions marred by the blacksmith's knife or nails, nor have his morals been corrupted by intercourse with jockeys, or his self-respect impaired by bad oats or corn. Such is the companion I have chosen for my journeyings, and, in case of danger, I must depend upon his legs for safety, for I have no means of defence.

Early on the 4th inst., I took leave of my friends at Port Lavacca. Major G., the grey-haired Texan who sold me my horse, was there to see me start, and to give me some counsel, and selected for me a Mexican saddle, such as are generally adopted here. I placed a loose coffee sack next to the horse's back, as he said, to prevent "scalding," then, a pair of blankets, and upon these the saddle, strongly girted, and over this a surcingle. A hair rope, about six rods long, called a *cabris* [*cabestro?*], to stake out the horse in the grass, a pair of saddle-bags, and a great coat lashed to the saddle, completed my equipage. I rode some miles to a line of trees marking the course of the Chocolate Creek.[3] Notwithstanding that it had not rained for more than four months, the grass here was rank and of a bright green, and the flowers, though few, were showy. Two species of the mimosa, or sensitive plant, were plentiful, one bearing a red, the other a yellow, flower. The clouds which overcast the sky when I started, broke away, about nine o'clock, into floating fragments, and the sun shone down with great power. Cattle, with unusually large horns, and very docile, were scattered about, and ash-colored doves flew up at every few paces. These are called coro camino by the Mexicans, and are very numerous. They closely resemble the turtle dove, and when one is on a tree alone, it utters the same plaintive note that the turtle does.[4] There were meadow-larks identical in appearance with those in the northern States, and towards evening they seem determined to attract attention, flying before the traveller from one dead stalk to another, uttering, as it alights, a strain

---

[3] Probably Chocolate Bayou, which rises in northwestern Calhoun County and flows southeastward twelve miles to empty into Chocolate Bay, about one mile south of Port Lavaca. *Ibid.,* I, p. 343.

View of Indianola, from the Bay, September 1860

From a lithograph by artist Helmuth Holtz on board the Barque *Texana*.

Courtesy of Eugene C. Barker Texas History Center, University of Texas, Austin

Frederick Law Olmsted and his brother, John, preferred camping out.
Primitive conditions in Texas hotels led Stillman to do the same.
Frontispiece from Olmsted's *Journey Through Texas*. Courtesy of Eugene C. Barker
Texas History Center, University of Texas, Austin

so sad, that you wonder if it is not tired of living on these prairies. The soil is a black loam, fissured everywhere by the drought, and bearing deep impressions of cattle's feet made during the rains. The roads, at such times, must be very heavy. I stopped a short time at the house built by Dr. Taylor,[5] who died at Port Lavacca two years since. It is built on piles ten or twelve feet from the ground, as a protection from the malaria, and surrounded by a grove of live oaks, which, at the moment, were filled with blackbirds, and the garden attached was hedged in by thrifty osage orange. I spent an hour in conversation with the intelligent lady of the house, after which I resumed the same obscure trail I had been following, until the grove I had left sunk below the horizon, and I was in a sea of green, on which cattle were no longer to be seen, no tree for shelter, or stream for refreshment—the sun all the time pouring down a blistering heat upon horse and rider, until the horizon dances from its effect.

---

[4] Texas had been noted for its bird life ever since Jean Louis Berlandier, Thomas Drummond, and John James Audubon had visited during the 1820s and '30s. Additional naturalists and scientists investigated the plant and animal life of the state during the following two decades, including the engineers, scientists, and artists of the United States and Mexican Boundary Survey. Audubon's famous study, *The Birds of America* (Edinburgh and London: J. J. Audubon, 1827-1838), contained many birds native to Texas, although none were drawn from Texas specimens because his visit came too late for them to be included. (The only bird that Audubon did from a Texas specimen was the Texan Turtle Dove, which was included in John James Audubon, *The Birds of America, From Drawings Made in the United States and Their Territories*, vols. 1-5 [N. Y: J. J. Audubon; Philadelphia: J. B. Chevalier, 1840-1842] vols. 6-7 [N.Y.: J. J. Audubon, 1843-1844], VII, opp. p. 352, plate 496.) Many of the birds gathered on the ensuing government surveying expeditions appeared in John Cassin, *Illustrations of the Birds of California, Texas, Oregon, British and Russian America* (Philadelphia: J. B. Lippincott & Co., 1856), and William H, Emory, *Report on the United States and Mexican Boundary Survey*, 34th Cong., 1st Sess., H. E. D. 135, 2 vols. (Washington: A.O.P. Nicholson, 1857, 1859), II, Pt. 2.

[5] There are only two Taylors listed in the 1850 census for Calhoun County, neither of them a doctor. See V. K. Carpenter (ed.), *The State of Texas, Federal Population Schedules: Seventh Census of the United States* (Huntsville, Ark: Century Enterprizes, 1969), I, pp. 272, 275.

Yet is the prairie no desert—one sees many familiar faces among the flowers there, and the chirp of the cricket, and the locust, sound as familiar as if you were harvesting in our northern fields. The night-hawk, startled from its covert, soars blindly into the sunlight—the whistling of the swift wing of turtle doves—the startling whirr of the grouse, and uninterrupted songs of larks and sparrows, all were sounds so familiar as to make me forget that I was on the borders of the torrid zone. Nor was I altogether unobserved, for, wherever I cast my eyes, the red deer were watching me, but so distant, that one seeing them, for the first time, could not be sure they were deer without a glass, but by its aid, I could distinguish the horns plainly. As I rode along, a fawn started from the long grass, where its mother had left it, probably, to go for water, and the sight of the beautiful creature bounding away before me, so animated me, that I started Pelicano in pursuit, without any intention, however, of catching the animal, but the horse had been reared to the chaise [*sic*], and went in to win. For a while it was an even race, but the fawn began to lag, and we were close upon it, when it doubled, and Pelicano shot by it so far that, before I could turn him again, the fawn was almost out of sight. These evolutions were repeated, until the fawn, exhausted, lay down, and Pelicano stood astride of it—when, dismounting, I took it up and threw it across the saddle, too weary to make any resistance. It was a beautiful creature. It made no effort to escape, but lay panting before me, its black eyes turned to me so gently—its well turned head and limbs so expressive of innocence and grace, that, instead of being the capturer, I was captivated. I was perplexed to determine what to do with it— should I carry it to the next ranch, about six miles further on? It might subject it to cruelty, and, perhaps, death. I had carried it about a mile, when it made a slight effort to escape, and, at the same time, uttered a cry so human, that it pierced my very soul, and I removed all restraints from it. With a bound it struck the turf, and was away retracing its step. "Go!" I said, "make the best of your brief life—the white man is on your track, a foe more ruthless than the savage—this kills only to supply his wants, but that destroys to gratify a passion." About the middle of the afternoon I halted at a little well, dug at the base of a sandy knoll, and, having staked out Pelicano to browse, I posted myself under the shade of a live oak. I had ridden eighteen miles, and was anxious to find the house at which I was advised to spend the first night. The prairie was more rolling than that portion which I had passed; and, in the vicinity of the Guadaloupe [*sic*]⁶ little sandy knolls, destitute of grass, offered as compensation fine clusters of oak and hackberry trees. The live oaks grow to a large size, with branches much knarled, and draped with the Spanish moss in large masses, hanging not only from the twigs, but from all the large branches, in many places completely concealing the limbs, except from below. The moss, like the bark, is of a light grey. I stopped that night at an inn kept by a widow lady and her sons.

I resumed my way at a late hour the next morning, in order to favor the horse, and because I also was not a little wearied. My road led through a low bottom, with coarse grass and rushes, some prickly pears, with flowers, orange-colored, striped with red like a bizarre tulip, then into a thicket of a great variety of trees, of which I recognized none as species common to the north, though many, if not all, belonging to genera commonly distributed. I noticed the sycamore, three species of the elm, one of maple, and four of oak. In one respect only, does the forest take a tropical aspect, and that is in the number of climbers and vines that hang on the trunks of the trees, and often load down their tops. These, with the Spanish moss, gives

---

⁶ The Guadalupe River rises in Kerr County and flows through Kendall, Comal, Guadalupe, Gonzales, De Witt, and Victoria counties, before pouring into San Antonio Bay. Webb, Carroll, and Branda (eds.), *Handbook of Texas*, I, pp. 743-44.

[*sic*] a very singular effect to the scenery. I crossed the bed of a stream, nearly dry now, but showing that the bottom is subject to inundations [*sic*], and as I rode in, a huge blue heron, fishing in a muddy pool near by, rose and flapped away into security. He need not have troubled himself—I did not come to destroy. Leaving this thicket, whose shade had been very grateful to me for an hour, the road skirted a beautiful prairie about four miles long, and two broad, whose clayey soil, of a dark blue color, was covered with a growth of grass green as young corn, but was entirely devoid of living inhabitants—not a moving creature was to be seen on it, save my horse and myself. I reached the Guadaloupe about noon. It is there about thirty yards wide, and flows with a speed of about five miles an hour, and turbid with the clay of its banks, which were overhung with willows. I spent the heat of the day sitting on the river bank, watching the fish playing and pursuing each other, listening to the songs of many strange birds, brushing the little black flies from my face, and drinking tepid water from the river. I am startled by the humming bird, which shoots by like an Indian's arrow, and high up, the vulture, with wing feathers spread like the fingers of an open hand, sails in majestic circles; for the vulture family, though obscene and disgusting birds on the ground, are unsurpassed in the grace and ease of their flight. They seem to have studied great circle sailing. Pelicano bites alternately the grass and the great green flies that are biting him, and waits my motions.

About three o'clock I resaddled, and ascended an abrupt elevation of about one hundred feet, to an extensive prairie extending further than the eye could reach.[7] The soil was a dark loam, with fresh water bivalves of the genus anodonta

---

[7] The bluff was probably Kemper's Bluff, located near a small community called McFaddin. Notes by Kathryn Stoner O'Connor, 302 East Red River Street, Victoria, Texas 77901, June 3, 1974; Webb, Carroll, and Branda (eds.), *Handbook of Texas,* I, p. 945.

showing in the water-worn ravines. Here was the cabin of the man who keeps the ferry.[8] Many cattle were scattered over the prairie, and droves of horses and herds of deer were always in sight. The scene was so novel and beautiful, that I paid too little attention to the road, which was but a trail or bridle-path, and as the sun went down, I could see no signs of a settlement, while the continued presence of deer made me fearful that I should be compelled to pass the night on the plain. I concluded to push on for a clump of trees to the left, and was urging my horse to a gallop, when I saw a solitary horse and rider on the horizon, just where the sun had gone down. I rode towards him, and when I had approached within hailing distance, he called to me—"Well, Dr., how do you fare on God's prairies." He was a man whom I had met at Port Lavacca, and was going back to that place. He directed me to follow the path till I found one leaving it at right angles, which would lead me to the house of a Mr. Cromwell.[9] I hurried on until it was so dark that I could no longer see the path, when I gave up all hope of finding a house. I looked for something to fasten the horse to, but not a stake or bush was in sight. I would have laid down and held the horse, so that he might graze, but I knew that in spite of our new-formed mutual regard, he would escape if I fell asleep, and if I tied him to my foot, he might, in case of fright, injure me severely. I had no choice but to travel. At length I discovered, by deepening twilight, a bush, but proceeding toward it, discovered that it grew from the side of a

---

[8] Probably Cromwell's Ferry, belonging to Judge A. H. Cromwell of Kemper's Bluff. It was located where U. S. Highway 77 from Victoria to Refugio now crosses the San Antonio River. Notes by Kathryn Stoner O'Connor in Victor M. Rose, *A Republishing of the Book Most Often Known as Victor Rose's History of Victoria,* edited by J. W. Petty, Jr. and Mrs. O'Connor (Victoria: Book Mart, 1961), pp. 25, 29.

[9] Judge A. H. Cromwell, who was born in Logan County, Kentucky, May 17, 1811, and moved to Texas in 1842. He settled near the San Antonio River in Victoria County. He served as a county commissioner and justice of the peace, and was, for a while, postmaster of Anaqua. He died December 2, 1872. *Ibid.,* pp. 110-11.

ravine, and was unapproachable.[10] One who has been thus alone in a strange, wild prairie, will understand my feelings. It grew very dark, and the fire-flies flashed around me as if in merry mockery, only making the way more dark. The night-hawk swooped down to me with a sound that I interpreted to be a prolonged boo-oo, and I plodded along cautiously, leading the horse. I thought I discovered a house, but on approaching it, found it to be a cluster of small trees. Here was a fastening point, but now I concluded to keep on still further. I seemed to be on the summit of a declivity, and peered earnestly, along the undistinguishable horizon, but as I walked along, could not perceive that my steps descended. I was still on the summit, and the prairie led down every way from me. At length I caught a glimpse of a light, and as I approached it I heard the sound of a handmill. I soon distinguished a cluster of huts, and let Pelicano into the enclosure. Several negroes appeared and took my horse, when I found that I had, as it were by chance, stumbled upon the place I was in search of, but which I sup-posed I had passed hours before. Mr. Cromwell had also been belated[ly] looking for cattle, and had but just returned to a late supper, which I was happy to be permitted to share with him.

J.D.B.S.

---

10 Probably the Ky Creek. Notes by Kathryn Stoner O'Connor.

The Crayon (New York), II (July 11, 1855), pp. 17-20.

Wanderings in the Southwest
No. II

San Antonio, June 1st, 1855.

I wrote in my last of my arrival at the town of Anaqua,[1] the residence of Mr. Cromwell and family, black and white. Mr. C. is chief magistrate, post-master, and the only free white man in the place, which, with one exception, is the smallest place that I ever saw; that was a town in Georgia, where the cars stopped a moment, and I was unable to institute any comparison, for it was fastened with a padlock. I was glad to find a place where I could sleep under a roof, for it seemed a severe trial to lay down under the open sky on the bare ground, where I had heard there were so many poisonous insects and reptiles, but I had something to learn. The sun had risen before me the next morning, when I strolled down to the San Antonio River.[2] It is here about one half the size of the Guadaloupe, where I crossed it the day before. In other respects, the characteristics are much the same—turbid, winding, with a current of above five miles an hour. Its channel is about fifty feet below the level of the prairie, and the banks, often precipitous, where the water has undermined them, show sand, with a deep, blank alluvium overlying it, and containing shells of Anodonta, Bulime and Helices of species now living, and found in great abundance on the uplands. I have seen no pebbles or stone as yet, in Texas.

---

[1] Probably the first site in Texas to receive a name, Anaqua on the San Antonio River in southern Victoria County, was the home of the Anaqua Indians that Alvar Nuñez Cabeza de Vaca described. It was a thriving settlement until the St. Louis, Brownsville and Mexico Railroad built five miles east and drew away much of the population. Webb, Carroll, and Branda (eds.), *Handbook of Texas*, I, p. 43.

[2] The San Antonio River flows through Wilson, Karnes, and Goliad counties after rising north of San Antonio. It forms the boundary between Victoria and Refugio counties en route to its confluence with the Guadalupe. *Ibid.*, II, pp. 544-45.

Grapes of three species I saw growing on its banks, and the pecan tree, I saw here for the first time. It is a tree very much resembling the pig-nut hickory of the North, but its branches make an angle more acute, and arched like the elm. Of the elm I saw three species.

I spent most of the forenoon on the banks of the river, shadowed by the moss-draped trees, and lulled by the murmur of the water among the fallen trunks. The cardinal grosbeak showed its scarlet plumage in the light green of the willow that dabbled its leaves in the river just where it took a short turn under a high, thicket-crowned, caving bank. A negro came down with two fish-lines, with enormous hooks, and after baiting them with the entrails of a fowl, he drove the sharpened ends of the poles into the bank, and sat down to wait the result. "What sort of fish do you catch here?" I asked. "Cat, sah." "No other kind do you catch in dis river?" "Oh, yes, sah, buffalo-fish, but dem we don't catch." Soon the fellow drew out a cat-fish, weighing about six pounds, of a species he called the yellow cat, and soon after I helped him with the other line to another of smaller size, which he called the blue-cat. The river abounded, he said, in gars and alligators, and no one dared to bathe in it. Mr. C. moved from East Tenn. three years since, is well satisfied with the country, has had less sickness than in Tennessee.[3] He has a very good garden, and his table at dinner was well supplied with peas, beans and beets, and it was but the fourth of May. He told me that the Irish potatoe, though it grows well, loses its eyes after the third year, and it is necessary to use new stock from the North. He showed me the persimmon tree, which grows here twenty feet high. The anaqua tree bears a berry about as large as a garden currant, and much esteemed for food. These trees grow in clusters on the prairies

---

[3] Stillman is obviously mistaken about the details of Cromwell's life. See Petty (ed.), *Some Historical Facts*, p. 110.

bordering the streams, in company with the hackberry, are generally of the same height, and unite their tops so close as to appear like one tree with many trunks. These furnish a grateful shade for cattle. Sometimes the oaks are found grouped in this way, and they are all known as "motts" in this country. A little boy brought to me the passion flower (*P. incarnata*), which seems to be spread widely over the country on the borders of the prairies. The root of a shrub called the Spanish apple was shown to me. It is long and succulent, and may be almost entirely reduced to a paste by pounding. It is much esteemed as an emolient application as a substitute for slippery elm, and I do not doubt could be used as a valuable article for the sickroom. After dinner I resumed my journey. The road led up the left bank of the river, but far enough from it to avoid the ravines and wooded bottoms. The rich, level prairie is left on the right, and here it is rolling and interspersed with "motts" and trees as tastefully as they could be arranged by Art, and it was so decidedly English that it would not have been difficult to have fancied that I stood on Hampstead heath again, and was looking off towards Highgate.

There are no wild cattle on these prairies; they are all thoroughly domesticated, and are often quite indisposed to get out of your path. The droves of horses, though no less sleek and gentle, seem to have less intertia to overcome. An ass and her hopeful full-grown, burly-headed son plant themselves by the path, and regard you with a curiosity so green as to make you laugh. I was passing a pond of standing water; the road led along that side of it which had been in more prosperous times its outlet, and I turned my horse's head to go around it. It was the first and the last collection of standing water I have seen in Texas. Alders grew in the mud, on the west side, and blackbirds were holding a convocation there, with a solemn white crane (*ardea occidentalis*), perched upon a tree in the centre as a presiding elder. I thought of an ornithological friend in New York who wished the skin of that very bird, and was sorry it was so inconvenient for him to get it. Plover were feeding along the margin of the water, and they seemed to know I had no gun; at a ravine, green and smooth, was an another [*sic*] assemblage of cattle. I have not seen as many grouse or prairie fowl as I expected, but this is their breeding season, and they have left for parts unknown. The cactus (*opuntia*) shows itself in the sandy margins of the motts where the red-ants have prepared the soil for them. As the sun went down, its low horizontal rays threw into relief the undulations of the prairie, with the deeper valleys in shadow running into the somber green of the river bottoms. I thought I never saw a landscape more harmonious. There seemed to be nothing out of place, not a bush or weed, not a dead leaf or dry blade of grass was anywhere to be seen. All was young, strong life, just passing into the "twilight of repose." I could but pause on the brow of a hill and wonder that so beautiful a scene should be without human habitation, and that fire and flood had made it what is was. It was nearly dark when I reached the domicile I had been looking for.[4] It was built like an overseer's house, two cabins under one roof, a popular style in Texas, and one which gives a fine space under cover, yet open to the breezes, and there the table is set. This serves as a general assembly-room. Sometimes it has floor, oftener not.[5] The proprietor was an old Texan, and his son, now seventeen years of age, was a

---

[4] The cabin probably belonged to Thomas O'Connor, who had one in that area. Notes by Kathryn Stoner O'Connor. For Thomas O'Connor, see Webb, Carroll, and Branda (eds.), *Handbook of Texas*, II, p. 301; Sister Margaret Rose Warburton, "A History of the O'Connor Ranch, 1834-1939" (Unpublished M. A. Thesis, Catholic Univ. of Amer., Washington).

[5] The style Stillman refers to is the "dog-run," or double log cabin type so common throughout the state. The house consisted of the two rooms and a ten-to-fifteen-feet passageway called a dog-run. Drury Blakely Alexander, *Texas Homes of the Nineteenth Century* (Austin: Univ. of Tex. Press, 1966), pp. 12-13.

native of the State.[6] Cotton had been grown in a field adjoining the State [ranch?], but it did not turn out a profitable
crop, and his attention was directed exclusively to stock, of
which he had about two thousand head. He was living with
but few comforts, you would say with but few necessaries. In
a cabin adjoining the one I have mentioned, a wretched hovel,
lived a large family of blacks, and in the evening the males
danced a "break-down" for our amusement, while the females,
made visible by the flame of a small fire on the heath, sat on
the ground, not seemingly to take any interest in the "fun."
When I rose the next morning a heavy fog enveloped the
place. I saddled my horse, and, waiting for breakfast, took a
look at the premises. Two black pigs, a strutting turkey, and
an old calico dress, were in the yard, and some fine peach trees
in the garden, with an acre or two of thrifty looking corn
beyond.[7] They had not attempted to raise garden vegetables.

The fog was lifting from the ground, but the crystal drops
were thick upon the grass, when I was again in the saddle.
Many deer were near the road, and two allowed me to approach
within two hundred yards of them. I left the straight road to
follow the winding of the river. I crossed a stream of clear
water running over a sandy bed, with fragments of rock from
limestone beds, which here have been exposed by the running
water. My horse took deep draughts, and when he had finished I did likewise. The banks were high, and the trees that
grew at the water's edge had masses of rubbish in their tops,
borne there by floods. I could not determine so well to-day the
course of the river by the trees, for the whole country seemed
to be covered with them, and the larger growth of the pecans,
poplars, and elms, which grow only along water-courses, were

---

6 The son was Dennis Martin O'Connor. Webb, Carroll and Branda, (eds.), *Handbook of Texas,* II, p. 300.

7 Thomas O'Connor kept a fine peach orchard. Notes by Kathryn Stoner O'Connor.

obscured by smaller trees growing on higher ground. It was necessary therefore, to travel as near as I could by the compass. This brought me again to the bank of the stream I had just crossed. A large turtle with a thin shell (*T. Ferox*), paddled with much noise over a wet sand-bar into deeper water, and two black ducks were floating in the shadow of a limestone ledge. The soil appeared not so good, grass was thinner, and flowering plants more abundant, the motts are more numerous and of smaller growth, degenerating into thickets. The carcass of a grey wolf lay in my way. The scenery changed to an oak opening with trees from eighteen inches to two feet in diameter, and from 30 to 50 feet high. I passed a spring, the rocks in which were stained white with sulphur, and around which many doves were gathered to drink.

About half-past ten the sun shone so hot that I was induced to tie my horse by the cabris [*cabestro*] to the branch of a tree, and lay down in the shade. It was one of those rare occasions which I have seen in Texas, when there was no refreshing breeze, and which, so far as my observation goes, indicates a storm. Not a cloud appeared to move, or leaf to stir upon the trees; invisible sparrows were singing; I heard the forsaken dove calling in its plaintive note, and the buzz of the horse-fly, that pesty little cosmopolite. A little way off comes an agitation in the grass, and a whirling of the dried leaves. I step out into the miniature whirlwind, and I have to hold my hat on my head; by and by it moves on and dies out, when it is as still and fiery as before. As I had designed to dine at Goliad,[8] I was forced to resume the journey, hot as it was. The scenery here loses its prairie character, although the term prairie does not seem to be used in the same restricted sense that it is in many

---

[8] The county seat of Goliad County, Goliad is one of the oldest cities in the state. The site of a Spanish mission and presidio, it was occupied largely by Anglo-Americans who moved the townsite to the opposite side of the San Antonio River after the Texas Revolution. Webb, Carroll and Branda (eds.), *Handbook of Texas,* I, p. 699.

parts of the great valley; but of the general topography of the country, I shall write in future. The surface is more rolling, limestone crops out of the hill-sides, whose surfaces are covered with scrubby bushes eight or ten feet high, thorny, small leaved, and of a great variety of forms. Among them, I saw one which bears a berry in color like the red currant, and of a very agreeable flavor; they crowd the branches in umbells, and are gathered by placing a sheet under the bushes and beating them. Its leaves are prickly, like the holly, and its wood is a fine yellow dye. On a hill commanding a view of the old city and mission buildings,[9] and a region of country of many miles in extent, stands the newly-erected academy.[10] Here I saw the first muskeet [*sic*] trees, which form so important a feature in the landscape of western Texas. It appears to be an acacia, closely resembling the thorny locust in foliage, being thin, and of a light green, but the branchlets were drooping like a willow. It branches low, and is generally deformed by prairie fire or storms. It is very brittle, but is said to be almost imperishable by decay. It is rare to find it exceeding a foot in diameter, but in favorable localities it will attain twice that size. Goliad, the new town on the left bank of the San Antonio, has a very thrifty appearance; the houses are mostly built of a yellow sandstone, containing lime.[11] But little attention has been paid to the cultivation of the ground, and few of the houses have gardens attached. I stopped at the only hotel in the place.[12] The county court was sitting, and at the moment of my arrival, were

9 The presidio and mission of La Bahía, more properly known as Nuestra Señora de Loreto Presidio and Nuestra Señora del Espíritu Santo de Zuñiga Mission are the ruins referred to by Stillman. *Ibid.*, II, pp. 293-94.

10 Aranama College and Paine Female Institute both operated in Goliad by the time Stillman visited there. He probably refers to Aranama College, which was founded in 1852 by William C. Blair. The Paine Female Institute was also founded in 1852 by the Methodist Episcopal Church. *Ibid.*, I, pp. 56, 699; II, pp. 324-25.

11 The houses were mostly built from the ruins taken from the presidio and mission. Notes by Kathryn Stoner O'Connor.

at dinner, so that I waited for the second table. I did not wait long; the company soon filled the porch where I was sitting. A more motley company could hardly be imagined, and costumes to match—silk stove-pipe hats, black Kossuth hats, white ditto, straw, palm-leaf, and Panama, and no hats; one lights a cigar, another a pipe. A huge fellow with black broad-brimmed hat, and hickory shirt all unbuttoned, and blue cotton pants well buttoned, is saluted as judge; he turns around exposing a bronzed face, neck, and bosom, and takes out a large double edged knife, with which he proceeds to pry the vension from between his teeth. There was something in his *tout ensemble* that excited my admiration. Quite other-wise was it with the man who addressed him, a miserable caricature of gentility, who had not sense enough to see that all his affectation of professional dignity, and his offcast costume of conventional life, were entirely out of place.

The dinner table was well supplied with meats, but there were no vegetables. I left Goliad with the intention of reaching a house nine miles distant, where I could pass the night. I was soon after joined by several men journeying the same way, and had gone about seven miles through a charming, rolling country, with rich grass and frost-oaks, when my companions stopped by a log cabin, with a fine corn-field adjoining. I inquired how much further it was to the terminus of my day's journey, when they told me that I had taken the wrong road, that this was the "settlement road," and that I must return. I inquired whether I could not find my way by striking a given course. I could, in about four miles, reach the San Antonio road by a direction which he indicated with his hand. The sun was about an hour high, and clouds were rising from the west to meet it. I rode fast through a country where there was no obstruction, over

---

[12] The only hotel keeper listed for Goliad in the 1850 census was J. M. Stoddard, age 50, from Connecticut. Carpenter (ed.), *Texas Federal Population Schedule*, II, p. 843.

hills and through valleys which vied with each other in beauty, and only deviated from the direction given, to avoid the branches of the oaks, until it began to grow dark, and flashes of lightening [*sic*] alternated with the rumble of the threatening storm. I thought I had gone twice the distance required to find the road, but I had seen no traces of man. I saw cattle, but they were astonished to see me there, and fled with their tails in the air; a herd of deer started up before me, and seemed less wild than the cattle; they would allow me to get near them, and running a few rods, would face about and present a front of bristling horns, and again I would see a line of white tails bobbing in the gloom. I was convinced, that by following the direction of the clouds when other things had failed me, I had lost my course. The storm had shifted more to the west, it grew very dark, and the frequent flashes of lightning only blinded me. I dismounted, and led my horse, in order that I might not pass the road, until it began to rain. I had thought of the contingency of being compelled to spend the night alone in the wilderness, but now the necessity was upon me in its most appalling form.

I could no longer distinguish the road if I were crossing it. I found a small muskeet tree, to which I made the horse fast, and stripped him, for which he was very grateful, and rolled himself upon the grass. I cut off the ends of the branches, and drew the saddleblankets over the tree, and, placing the saddle in the crotch, I mounted it, and for a moment felt that I was well protected from the rains above and the wolves below; but I was soon made aware that it was not a position for repose, it was but a prolongation of the labors of the day, while the woolen canopy made it oppressively warm. Something stung me on the leg, and I crushed the offender, which I think was a cantharis, for the crushed insect retaliated by blistering me the next day, wherever it touched my skin in its descent, as thor-

oughly as could be done by the official preparation. I endured
my position as long as possible. I could hear no sound of wolves,
nor the growl of a panther, and the rain did not come very
hard, while the thunder and lightning grew more distant; at
the same time I felt that overpowering tendency to sleep that
made it imperative upon me to lie down: so I spread the blanket upon the ground, placed my saddle for a pillow, and fell
asleep listening to Pelicano cropping the grass. Once he awaked
me by laying down too familiarly near me; all was silent but
the sound of the mocking bird, and I thought I never heard
anything so melodious, as it warbled on in the still night, while
the stars were shining out where the dark clouds had been. It
was cooler, and I wrapped my coat close about me and laid
down again. In the morning, I found that I had crossed the
road, and a Mexican cart had stopped for the night not far off.
I lost that night my fear of "camping out" alone, and I prefer
to so now to staying in the houses of the settlers.

It is said that a bad wife makes a man an early riser, and I
am sure that such an infliction would not be necessary, were we
always to make our bed upon the ground, with the saddle for
a pillow, and a single blanket to lie upon. I rose with the first
dawn much refreshed, and my horse was surfeited with the
rich muskeet grass, which I saw now for the first time. A
ride of two miles brought me to a small stream of clear water,
where I drew out of my saddlebags the last two biscuit [*sic*]
placed there by a friend at Lavacca, to meet emergencies. Soak-
ing them in water, I breakfasted, and drank the brook water
from my hand. I found the house I was in search of the night
before, but the men had gone a-fishing. The country over which
I rode this morning was less picturesque; the swells, to use a
nautical term, were longer, trees fewer or degenerated into
clumps of muskeet bushes not sufficient for shade, but the soil
is rich and covered with a good growth of grass. At eleven

o'clock, I reached a valley with a dry creek and live oaks. Here I rested an hour, to favor the horse, and climbed one of the oaks with my note-book, to enjoy the shade and breeze. During the afternoon the scenery was much the same, rich soil, good grass—little timber, no water. The sun was low, when the sight of a cornfield indicated the habitation of a white man. There was a duck pond from which my horse drank heartily, the ground was miry about it, and grass, the yellow pond lily (nuphar), and sagittaria were growing in it. I went to the house, and found there only a woman and her two children; her husband was out hunting cattle. I represented to her that I was very hungry and thirsty; but she kept on sewing and all appeals to her humanity were ineffectual. Her husband was not at home, and that was sufficient for her. At last I requested her little daughter to bring me a glass of water, which she did —and, though I knew it came from the mud-hole from which my horse just drank, I swallowed it, and travelled six miles further to the Clito Creek.[13]

This is a pretty stream with wooded bottoms, and a log cabin stood on its further bank, at which I applied for admission. The man who lived in it was not the owner, but was cultivating a corn-field on shares; he was poor, and owned but twenty cows. A thunder-shower was approaching, and I waited till it should pass; in the meantime, a meal was prepared, which quite reconciled me to my situation. When the rain had passed, it was quite night, and the road so wet that I determined to stay here for the night, though I had it in my programme to stop at a new town called Helena.[14] The rain-water was many degrees cooler than any water I have drank in the country. I caught a pitcher full, as it ran in generous streams from the

---

[13] Clito (Cleto) Creek flows southward from Guadalupe County into Wilson and Karnes counties, then into the San Antonio River. See *Johnson's New Map of the State of Texas* (N.Y: Johnson Browning, [1861]). See James M. Day (comp.), *Maps of Texas, 1527-1900* (Austin: Pemberton Press, 1964), p. 69; Webb, Carroll and Branda (eds.) *Handbook of Texas,* I, pp. 540-541.

roof of the cabin, and drank enough; and, when I remembered the burning thirst with which I had ridden all day, and the duck pond, I drank more, and filled the pitcher to place where I could get it in the night. A low thicket grew on the creek in the rear of the house, whence wolves and other wild animals make forage upon the young stock. The pigs had all been destroyed this year, and a panther was seen but the day before. An excellent bed was furnished me, and my apartment, which was half of the house, was dry. There was no window, but a short log had been left out where one was required, and everywhere from roof to floor were chinks open, revealing the lightning. I put my pitcher of pure, heaven-descended water in a rawhide bottomed chair, and went to sleep, with the deep bass music of the bull-frogs, rejoicing in the rain.

In the night I was awakened by the most infernal noises. The hogs had resorted to the space under the floor, just where my bed stood, in violation of the laws of the place, and were engaged in a free fight; the dogs soon joined in; this called out my host, and a long contest resulted in dislodging the hogs and restoring quiet. In the morning the rain still continued, or was renewed, and the air was cool. Mr. Reisinger[15] moved from Louisiana, where he lived four years, and . . . was compelled to leave in consequence of the continued illness of his family from intermittents, and has never had sickness in his family since his residence in Texas, now two years. From this place I rode four miles over a table-land of rich, dark loam, covered with muskeet trees and grass; the road was strewn with the

---

14 Established in 1852, Helena is located in central Karnes County. It was named after Helena Owens and designated the county seat in 1854. It was the main stop on the stage line connecting San Antonio with the coast. Webb, Carroll, and Branda (eds.), *Handbook of Texas*, I, pp. 793-94.

15 Probably J. W. Resinger, a thirty-eight year old stockraiser, who lived in Helena with his family in 1860. See "Population Schedule of the Eighth Census of the United States, 1860," Karnes County, p. 131. (Microfilm copy, Fort Worth Public Library).

broken trees from the gale of two nights before, which seemed
to have passed over this flat. In wet weather, long continued,
the roads must become almost impassable from mud; the alluvium is so fine and tenacious as to clog the wheels of carriages,
and cause animals to slip at every step. Where oaks are found, the
soil is more sandy. At Helena, which has been said to resemble
a settlement of disbanded rangers, I stopped a short time. A
group of young men of American parentage were lounging
about with revolvers at their belts; some were playing at bil-
liards, others were drinking at a bar, but I saw no garden or
enclosure about the town, and I felt to congratulate myself that
I did not reach this place so as to spend a night there. Seeing a
well recently dug on the high ground west of Helena, I had
the curiosity to dismount and inspect the formation of the soil.
The black loam was about eight feet deep, then pebbles, mostly
of flint, and a cretaceous mud, with a tinge of iron rust, containing nodules of chalk, down to the depth of forty feet. I
reached the Civolo [*sic*][16] about noon: there is much beautiful
land in this vicinity, very productive and well watered; there
are many settlements on the stream, and some have left it, because it was too crowded. The Civolo, like all the streams I
have crossed, runs through a deep valley, but at this season of
the year, it is but a brook, with clear good water. The view is
very picturesque at the ford, and I spent three hours there.
Pecans are the most numerous trees, and their fine foliage
keeps the water, for the most part, in shadow. I found here
some very large unios, the shells of which will weigh, at least,
a pound. They lie imbedded in mud, with the mouth of the
shell pointing down stream, and a little open, so that their food

---

[16] Cibolo Creek rises in southern Kendall County and flows southeastward, forming
the boundary between Bexar and Comal, Bexar and Guadalupe, and Guadalupe and
Wilson counties. It continues southward through Wilson and Karnes counties and empties into the San Antonio River near Karnes City. Webb, Carroll, and Branda (eds.),
Handbook of Texas, I, p. 347.

shall glide over the shell with the current, and, in dropping down the margin, they are caught within the two valves. There is a fine fish of the perch family found in all the streams that unite with the San Antonio and Guadaloupe—it is improperly called here trout; it sometimes attains the size of five or six pounds. There is, also, another of the same family very similar to the little pumpkin-seed or sun-fish, so common in the ponds of the North. I walked a little way down the margin of the stream, when a moccasin snake, partly concealed by a log, raised its flattened head, and opened its jaws so wide, as to put them almost in the same plane. I carried my foot close to it, and it struck its fangs into my boot. It is a very repulsive reptile, about eighteen inches long, and clumsy; it makes no attempt to escape, and is harmless to those who have boots, but it is very dangerous to those who are bare-footed, and women are sometimes bitten in the hand while getting water; it is widely diffused in the South, and is found only on the margin of watercourses. I have seen three varieties of it in Texas. On the opposite bank of the Civolo is an old Mexican ranch, the owners of which had just killed a calf, which was hanging to a tree; and, as I had not yet seen any meat of the kind in an American house, I was disposed to stop for the night, but could not speak their language. I stopped at a house on the Marcelina[s][17]—not a running stream there, but whose quicksands nearly proved the grave of my horse. The house was built of poles standing on end, after the Mexican style, but was occupied by a Missourian. I dined on the usual fare of bacon, corn bread, and fried eggs, and slept in a room with a curtain pinned up for a door. When I looked about me in the morning the room was occupied, beside myself, with two dogs, a family of chickens, two hand-saws, a deer-skin, and auger, and a spare-bed. I

[17] Marcelinas Creek is an intermittent stream that rises in central Wilson County and flows eighteen miles southward to the San Antonio River. *Ibid.,* II, p. 141.

was informed here of the settlement of Mr. Tentant, of Lou-
isania [*sic*], about six miles out of my way on the San Antonio;
and, being anxious to find an intelligent settler, who, from
experience, could tell me something of the results of the agricultural experiments of the country, I started at seven o'clock,
after paying the customary fee of one dollar for the hospitality
I had enjoyed, directing my course for some conspicuous trees
that I saw on a hill in the direction indicated; it led for a time
down the Marcelina, in the standing water-holes of which were
Mallard ducks and Mergansers, and great numbers of turtle.
Several times I saw deer, found a wagon trail, but could not
find the trees that were to be my landmark—followed the
wagon trail till I was sure it was leading me astray—rode to
the top of a high hill, and rode down again no wiser—travelled
four hours—came to the San Antonio River, but no ranch—
went down stream for a mile, and became tangled in a thicket
of bushes and giant weeds—saw a file of wild turkeys crossing
my path, was very glad to see them, and sorry I could not make
a more intimate acquaintance. I then ascended the river, which
was no where accessible, nor even visible, from the dense vegetation on its banks. There were some fine specimens of the
Turks-head cactus (*Echinocactus*) here, and the small variety
of the Yucca (*Yucca fillimentora*). I resolved that I was lost,
and abandoning all hope of finding Mr. T.'s ranch, I struck a
course due west for about six miles over deep valleys, and hills
commanding a wide view of the surrounding country, when I
saw a field that appeared of a fresher green than the adjacent
country. By the aid of my glass I distinguished the corn, and
made for it with more satisfaction than I could tell you, for I
had now no reserve biscuit in my saddle-bags, and I had given
up any hope of seeing a settlement that day. My surprise was
great, when I found that I was at Mr. T.'s place, which I supposed I had left somewhere twelve miles behind me. Mr. T.

lives in a style baronial; he had a young priest at his house, and a large number of blacks; deer skins were stretched to the trees, and horns were nailed up in several places. The room into which I was introduced, was decorated with guns, books, pictures, and pistols, and while we were talking, some fresh venison was being prepared for our dinner. The family had dined, and the priest and myself partook of a dinner together. Mr. T. had had his servants bitten with rattlesnakes, and to guard against them wore leather leggings. Mr. T. had not been long enough in the country to make any experiments; his attention was occupied in the cultivation of corn and other necessaries of life. He tills about 3,000 acres. He accompanied me on my way for two miles, and directed me to go to Mr. Flores'[18] ranch, where fruit had been cultivated for a long time. This I succeeded in reaching just at night-fall.

J.D.B.S.

---

[18] Flores probably is the family for whom Floresville was named, perhaps José M. Flores. See *ibid.,* I, p. 612; Carpenter (ed.), *Texan Federal Population Schedule,* I, p. 172.

The Crayon (New York), II (July 18, 1855), pp. 33-35.

Wanderings in the Southwest
No. III

From Mr. Barker, son-in-law to Flores, I received hospitality such as we might expect from old Texans. His garden is on a high bank of the San Antonio. Here were peach trees, large and very thrifty. Fig trees were killed by the unusually severe frost of the last winter. Sugar cane thrives well here. Before I slept, I brought the horse in from the grass, for fear of having him stolen by the vagrants that hang around old settlements, and an unsuccessful attempt was made to seduce him into eating corn. From this place, the old road up the river affords much picturesque scenery. Old Mexican ranches are frequent, the country is well wooded, and the trees often of large size; the pecan trees, especially, fill all the ravines where their roots can have access to water, and the mustang grape vine loads down their tops. In some places the country is very sandy, and there the oaks thrive well. The trees along the river are still draped with Spanish moss, but those away from it have another parasite with linear leaves, growing in clusters enveloping the branches. Occasionally the road leads along the crest of a ridge, looking over deep ravines on either hand, with the pecan trees growing in them, to the hills beyond, covered with oaks, so as almost to conceal the deeper green of the grass that covers the ground. I descended to the river for water, where the San Antonio tumbles over a ledge of limestone rocks. I passed several hawks, known here as Mexican buzzards. They have long bare legs, the feathers about the neck white, with a black crest like a cap projecting over their eyes; they are quite tame, and seem to be hunting about on the ground for reptiles. Another hawk, nearly white, with a long forked tail, passed over me.

Scarabeus [*sic*] beetles are very numerous, rolling little balls of their favorite composite, in the road. One species is extremely beautiful, with colors of green and gold. A ride of twenty-one miles brought me to Mr. Buquer's, whom I sought as an old resident of Texas, for such information as his experience could furnish.[1] He has a pleasant cottage, and his place evinces industry and taste. His peach trees were yellow, and his garden was nearly a failure from the want of rain. Though this disaster was unusual, still he said it had occurred several times since his residence of seventeen years in the country. He had made few experiments with fruit trees.

A tedious ride of nine miles over a plain of muskeet, brought me to the Silado [*sic*][2] creek, but it was so dark that I could scarcely find my way across it, and when I emerged from the shadow of the pecans, and ascended the high ground of the opposite bank, I could not distinguish one object from another. I expected to find the house of Gideon Lee,[3] of New York, and looked for a light to guide me to it, but I only saw the low growth of bushes along the road, and the innumerable fire-flies shooting athwart the gloom. There was distant thunder and lightning, and a little rain had fallen, which served to draw out these most interesting of all the numerous insects that swarm in hot climates. They were of several species of Eleteridae, and were so brilliant, that if they would but have kept over the road, I could not desire a better light. A single one would render everything visible for a rod about, but leave it darker than before. I caught one to force it into my service, but its light

---

[1] Perhaps Mr. Buquer was the P. L. Buquor who was elected county commissioner in Beat No. 1, Bexar County. *Alamo Star* (San Antonio), Oct. 9, 1854, p. 2, col. 1.

[2] Salado Creek rises in northern Bexar County and flows into the San Antonio River about five miles southeast of San Antonio. Webb, Carroll, and Branda (eds.), *Handbook of Texas,* II, p, 532.

[3] Gideon Lee, of New York, lived on Salado Creek in 1850. He was thirty years of age. Carpenter (ed.), *Texas Federal Population Schedule,* I, p. 183.

went out, it folded its legs up, and feigned death. In the distance they would shine so steadily for a time, as quite to deceive me with the idea that it was light in a human dwelling. I did see a light at length, at some distance on the right of the road, and directed my course towards it, but as the way led down hill, and the chance was, that it was on the opposite side of the creek, I retraced my steps, and dismounted, the more readily to find the road I had left, but all my efforts were in vain, and I was compelled again to tie my horse to a tree and lie down at the foot of it, which I did with a feeling of greater security, now that I was but six miles from San Antonio. I slept well, and rose early; found that it had rained during the night; saddled my horse, and having no toilet to make, was soon on my way. The country in the vicinity of San Antonio has not been burned over for some years, and the muskeet bushes have grown up everywhere, and if not cleared off, will soon be out of danger of fire. The soil is of a dark loam, with flint pebbles.

From the brow of a hill, I saw at length the white houses of San Antonio scattered through the green, three miles distant, and a quarry close at hand, from which a building material is taken. It is chalk, but so friable as scarcely to admit of handling, yet is used much from its being cheaper than the better qualities of stone. I soon passed through a double row of mud cabins, thatched with grass, and came upon the river—clear, swift, and sparkling.[4] It flowed through no deep channel, but

----

[4] Many visitors to San Antonio approached from this direction and reacted similarly to Stillman. Olmsted, *Journey Through Texas*, p. 149, commented upon them, as did John Russell Bartlett, *Personal Narrative of Explorations and Incidents in Texas, New Mexico, California, Sonora, and Chihuahua, Connected with the United States and Mexican Boundary Commission, During the Years 1850, '51, '52, and '53,* two vols. (New York: D. Appleton & Co., 1854), I, p. 38. This is the La Villita section of San Antonio, which has now been restored and is a popular tourist attraction. See Charles Ramsdell, *San Antonio: A Historical and Pictorial Guide,* 2nd rev. ed. by Carmen Perry with Charles J. Long (Austin: Univ. of Tex. Press, 1985), pp. 105-111.

river and channel just fitted each other. I wanted to water the horse, but felt some degree of delicacy about it, and paused for a moment upon the bridge. A copper-colored man, with broad brimmed, steeple-crowned hat, small moustache, shirt and pants, and a red sash, came down leading a horse to water; this removed all scruples, and I urged my pony to drink; but the sight was so new to him, that it was with difficulty that I could induce him to approach the margin. His thirst being satisfied, I rode along a narrow street, with low one story houses built close upon it, interspersed with some new stores in more modern style, and some delightful residences standing back from the street.

I stopped at a hotel kept by Mr. Reade, just in time for breakfast, after a journey of eight days from the coast, although the distance was less than two hundred miles. I shall write an account of this city when I come to speak of the topography of the country, and to give the general results of my journey. My trunks had not arrived, and therefore my letters were unavailable. I, however, called on Dr. Douai[5] of the *Zeitung,* who had been informed by Mr. Olmstead [*sic*] of my intended visit to this place, and at his office I also saw Mr. Riott. Both are men of high attainments, and with an undying love for that cause for which they are exiles. After two days' rest, I set out in company with Dr. Douai to visit Castroville,[6] a settlement of Alcestians formed nine years since. The distance was twenty-eight miles, and the road presented but little of special interest.

---

[5] Dr. Adolf Douai published the *San Antonio Zeitung,* the first German language paper in the city, beginning in July 1853. One of a number of German intellectuals who immigrated to Texas in 1848 and 1849, he published a literary and educational newspaper and espoused abolitionism. When he expressed his opinions too strongly, merchants withdrew their support from his newspaper. He was the object of numerous threats, but it was financial failure that forced him to sell his paper to Gustav Schleicher and leave Texas in 1855. Douai toured Olmsted around San Antonio and vicinity. Webb, Carroll, and Branda (eds.), *Handbook of Texas,* II, p. 547; Olmsted, *Journey Through Texas,* p. 187.

The grass was very good, and corn looked well. The settlements along this road are frequent. We cross several streams before we reach the Medina.[7] This is a fine stream, and a dam of superior construction has been thrown across it at Castroville. A good hotel is kept there by Mr. Tardé,[8] a Frenchman. The place has about 3,000 inhabitants, and is so remarkably healthy, that, as I was informed by the two physicians of the place, there had been but three deaths in a year. The population is very industrious and orderly, though far below the Germans in intelligence and enterprise.

Owing to the careless manner in which I saddled my horse, and fast riding, I injured him so badly that I did not deem it prudent to use him at once, and led him a few miles down the river where was good grass, and amused myself on the bank of the river. Large cypresses grew along the bank of this river, close to the water's edge, and grape vines whose trunks measured six or eight inches in diameter, loaded them down with their huge folds, the small light green leaves of the cypress contrasting finely with the large leaves and dark masses of the grape. After taking a bath, I seated myself in the shade of a pecan on a shelving bank, where a willow, inclined almost horizontally, trailed its branches in the water. The *smilax,* a bright leaved, thorny vine, common about New York, a dwarf black walnut,

---

[6] Founded by Henri Castro in 1844, Castroville is in Medina County some twenty-five miles west of San Antonio. See Bobby D. Weaver, *Castro's Colony: Empresario Development in Texas 1842-1865* (College Station: Tex. A&M Univ. Press, 1985), pp. 40-56.

[7] Rising in two branches in northern and western Bandera County, the Medina River flows across Bandera, Medina, and Bexar counties to join the San Antonio River about eight miles south of San Antonio. Webb, Carroll, and Branda (eds.), *Handbook of Texas,* II, pp. 168-69.

[8] V. Tarde ran the Castroville Hotel, which he said was in the "house lately occupied by H. Castro, Esq." *Western Texan* (San Antonio), Mar. 6, 1851, p. 3, col. 7. Beginning early in 1853, he advertised his "new and commodious house" with "stable and provender on the premises." *San Antonio Texan* Feb. 8, 1855, p. 5, col. 4. Olmsted also visited Tardés hotel. See Olmsted, *Journey Through Texas,* p. 277.

and many stranger shrubs surrounded me. The river at this place is deep, and thirty yards wide, and flows sluggishly, but below me I heard the murmur of a rapid sometimes blended with the sough of the wind amongst the trees, but never with the complaint of a mosquito. A mocking-bird alighted in a tree close over my head, to answer the song of his lady-love on the other side of the stream. A limb had concealed me from him for a while, but suddenly he stopped, with the notes of one of his sweetest impromptus in his throat, at the sight of a man in blouse taking notes; he stretched his neck to the utmost over the limb, first in one direction then in another; he seemed to say, "Oh, my eyes!" and hopping from one limb to another very quickly, he took wing. The water has a greenish transparency, and I see a perch gliding along as straight as if he were going to the post-office for a letter from home, yet stopping at the margin of a leaf of the pond weed to snap at a fly. A soft-shell turtle crawls timidly up the bank directly opposite me into a sunny spot, and begins to excavate a hole in the ground to deposit her eggs, by throwing the dirt out with her hind feet, using them alternately, and at each flirt throwing it some yards into the river, all the time looking very carefully about her, to be sure that no one shall be aware what she is about. She has chosen a place where cattle come down to drink, and a young steer appears through the bushes. The turtle makes a quick evolution, and plunges into the water. The steer, startled in his turn, looks with wonder and fear at the spot where he heard the plunge, and sees the water circling, looks back, and waits for reinforcements. Two, then three juvenile cattle put their heads together to solve the mystery, and finally seem to settle the matter, that there is no reasonable ground of apprehension, and go down to drink. I sat in the midst of this interesting society until the setting sun began to open fire upon my retreat.

Of the state of the settlements I shall be able to give a better account when I revisit the country west of San Antonio, which I shall do as soon as I am posted in my correspondence. I hope to go as far as Mexico, unless I am interrupted by new misfortunes. Returning, we started late to avoid the heat of the sun, and camped about ten miles from Castroville, in preference to sleeping in a house. My baggage not having yet arrived, and my horse being too sore to ride, I camped for three days about four miles down the river, on lands owned by Mr. Riott, enjoying myself much with my gun. Quails, rabbits, and grey squirrels are plenty, and milk and eggs were obtained at a house in the vicinity, and when night came, I followed the instinct of my horse, and went up on the high prairie, in the musqueet grass to sleep.

On the 21st of May, I left San Antonio for the settlements north of this place. The country, drained by the rivers Llano[9] and San Seba, [*sic*][10] had been represented to me as one of great interest, presenting a variety of formation from primary to tertiary, and abounding in valleys of great fertility and beauty. I left town in the evening, and camped near San Pedro Springs,[11] where there was good grass. The moon had gone down, and clouds shut out the stars. For more than an hour I searched for my bed: I thought I had not left it a rod, but I could not find it, and was forced to pull off my coat for a pillow, and renew my sleep on the grass. From the Springs northward the country becomes hilly, and the musqueet grass and trees which are almost

---

[9] The Llano River is formed from two main forks which join in Kimble County and flow through Mason and Llano counties to join the Colorado River in southeastern Llano County. Webb, Carroll, and Branda (eds.), *Handbook of Texas*, II, pp. 70-71.

[10] The San Saba River has three head streams that rise in eastern Schleicher County and unite in Menard County. The river flows through Mason and McCulloch counties to join the Colorado River in San Saba County. *Ibid.*, II, p. 562.

[11] Perhaps Stillman is referring to San Pedro Creek, which rises in central Bexar County and flows into the San Antonio River. *Ibid.*, II, p. 560.

invariably found together, give place to the coarser grass of the coast country. At this season of the year this grass is of a bright green, and gives a charm to the landscape. Later in the season, it becomes brown, and is burned over. The muskeet, on the contrary, is greenest in the winter, and is much relished by animals even in its dry state. I thought I should have no difficulty in finding a settlement at which to breakfast before I had travelled far, but after leaving the Springs, one mile from town, I saw no dwelling place of man until eleven o'clock. I was on the road to Fredericksburg,[12] and had ridden over a country which, could one be placed at once in it without having seen any intermediate places, would call out the most extravagant admiration. There was every variety of surface that was possible, without the turf being broken. In the deepest valley I did see the turf broken, and white chalk showing where the torrent had been most violent. But now there was no water for twelve miles, and then only at a well. I rode up to a cabin where a young man was skinning a deer, and proceeded without ceremony or invitation to unsaddle. A piece of that vension I meant to have. He referred me to the old man in the house, who, when I told him I had not yet breakfasted, asked me whether I would have breakfast or dinner! I told him I did not care by what name he called it, if there was only some venison in it. He was a middle-aged man, from Arkansas, and employed his time while talking with me, in striking at the chickens, dogs, and black children, who came unbidden into his presence. Just as dinner was announced, Mr. Tyson,[13] a German settler on the Upper Guadaloupe,[14] rode up and join-

---

12 Fredericksburg, Texas, in Gillespie County, was founded in 1846 by some settlers from New Braunfels, led by John O. Meusebach. *Ibid.,* I, p. 643.

13 Mr. Tyson, formerly a member of the Frankfort Parliament, had become relatively wealthy upon moving to Texas. His farm lay in a bend of the Guadalupe River. Olmsted, *Journey,* p. 194.

14 The north fork of the Guadalupe rises in Kerr County and unites with the south branch near Kerrville. Webb, Carroll, and Branda (eds.), *Handbook of Texas,* I, p. 743.

ed us. There were about five flaxen-haired children, and one sleeping in the cradle, five dogs, and three woolly heads, besides one of doubtful complexion. The charge of twenty-five cents for our meal we considered very moderate. Just as we left, we were reinforced by Judge Behr,[15] of Sisterdale,[16] and felt ourselves strong, though we were all unarmed. I have noticed that the German settlers generally go unarmed about the frontiers, while Americans uniformly carry revolvers, many even carry them wherever they go, just as a gentleman carries his watch, and they seem to think it as indispensable. I saw recently the impropriety of carrying pistols to evening parties, urged by a Texas paper. Soon after leaving this house, we entered the dry valley of the Leon.[17] Along the bed of the Leon is much limestone, and cliffs sometimes rise perpendicularly. The valley is narrow, bounded by hills rising several hundred feet, and many of them attaining to the dignity of mountains. They are mostly bare, or presenting here and there patches of small bushes, with horizontal ledges of limestone cropping out where some strata have been less easily broken down than the others, so as to give the appearance of terraces. Six miles brought us to the Leon Spring, the first good water we had found in eighteen miles, and this is but a small spring, whose supply is drank up by the thirsty earth in a short time. A German has opened a house of entertainment at this place, and supplies his table by his gun. Occasionally the valley spreads out into charming fields, with groves of post oak. This hilly region abounds everywhere with the white bundles of the flowers of the *Yucca fillamentosa.*

---

15 Judge Otto (Ottmar) von Behr, who came to Sisterdale in 1848, died on a return trip from Germany in 1855. See Olmsted, *Journey Through Texas,* p. 193; Chester W. and Ethel H. Geue (comps. & eds.), *A New Land Beckoned: German Immigration to Texas, 1844-1847,* (Waco: Texian Press, 1966) p. 155.

16 Founded in 1847, Sisterdale, Texas, is in Kendall County. It gets its name from Sister Creek, which is formed by several brooks called the Sisters. Webb, Carroll, and Branda (eds.), *Handbook of Texas,* II, p. 616.

17 Stillman is probably referring to an area near Leon Spring, Texas, a village in northwestern Bexar County. *Ibid.,* II, p. 49.

Leaving the valley of the Leon, we cross several small streams of good water, and rode over hills covered with live, and post oak, to the Civolo, a large and beautiful stream, which, a short distance below the crossing, tumbles down a chasm in the rocks, and does not appear again in forty miles. Of this curious phenomenon I shall have more to say when I speak of the general features of this region. There is a German settlement at this place; and, as it was dark on our arrival, we passed the night here, stabling the horses for fear of Indians. The following morning I left the Fredericksburg road, to accompany my friends to their settlement on the Guadaloupe. The country, for the most part, was rough, and the soil thin, although there were some pretty valleys with brooks of clear water. We made our way through thickets of shrubbery, and grape vines of a species that I had seen in the low country, but here in the mountains they are numerous, though vines and grapes are small.

Mr. Tyson, with a generosity as gratifying as unexpected, insisted upon my spending some weeks at his house, in which he appropriated the best room to my use. His farm is located on a bend of the river, so that he requires but one fence. He has a large corn-field under cultivation, and he has an abundance of timber of oak and cypress. The Guadaloupe here runs in a deep narrow channel cut in the limestone, and the cypress trees grow in the bed of the channel, just at the water's edge, their tops reaching above the bank. Some of these attain the size of five feet in diameter, and they form a row on each side of the water, that gives a very unique appearance to the river. There are no parasitic plants growing on the trees here. The water flows over a pebbly bed, and is so transparent, that you might find a needle on the bottom. We went down to the river to bathe soon after our arrival, and a greater luxury could not be furnished in the mountains. We drank while we swam, for

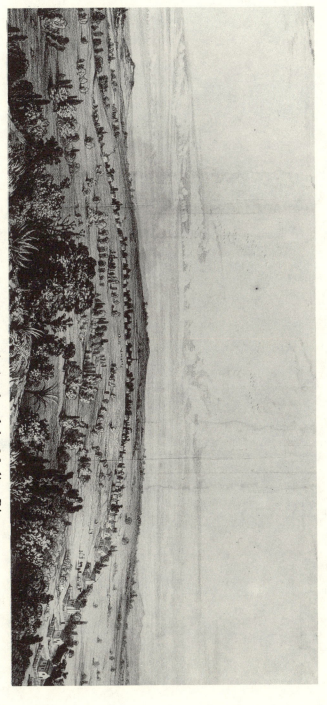

View of Castroville, 1845, on the banks of the Medina River

Drawn by Theodore Gentilz and published in Henri Castro *Le Texas in 1845: Castroville Colonie Française* (Anvers, 1845). Courtesy of Eugene C. Barker Texas History Center, University of Texas, Austin

Dr. Ernst Kapp's Water Cure, Comal County, Texas

On Sister Creek, a tributary of Guadalupe River, the professor moved his family here in an attempt to find the "perfect" life.

Lithograph after Hermann Lungkwitz, c. 1853. Courtesy of Roy O. Perkins and Ida B. Perkins

we knew that the water came to us pure. How many thousands of beings, human and other, does it supply, as it flows on for three hundred miles below, with the only drink they know during many months. It is curious to see the effect light has on the colors of fish. The same species of fish found below are here much more finely colored—and even the Cat-fish, of which I caught two, were covered with small, black spots.

With the exception of one settlement twelve miles higher up, Mr. Tyson's is the last on the Guadaloupe; though, for thirty miles, the character of the country continues much the same. The elevation cannot exceed seven or eight hundred feet above the sea, but the air is decidedly cooler, than fifty miles below. The best lands are held at $2 per acre. The land on the hills is valuable as a sheep range, and the bottoms and flat lands are equal to any in the State. I was at a loss to account for the cordiality with which I had been treated by the Germans with whom I had become acquainted, until I found it to be a general thing among all the better class of them, and there are many such here and all through western Texas. I could not speak their language; I had not even seen the land of the Rhine, but, if I had been familiar with both, they could not have treated me with more cordiality; and yet they are regarded by the great part of our countrymen, with a conceit only surpassed by their ignorance and ill-manners, as though they were little better than negroes. What a bitter disappointment it is to the cultivated German who lands upon our shores, expecting to find there the fruit of four score years of freedom maturing into justice, truth and generosity, and to find just the opposite! I have been in company with a room full of Germans, and there was not one of them who could not expound our Constitution and history better than I could. Yet to the mass of Americans whom I meet, they are d——d Dutch. Even their industry is made an object of jealousy. Two Americans were riding along the fence which encloses garden upon garden, and corn-field after corn-field, for nearly seven miles west of New Braunsfels [*sic*],[18] when one said to the other, "Bill, look what a fence these fellows have made—these G—d d——d Dutch-men." But, I am digressing. On the third day we took our horses to ride down to see Mr. Behr, who has a place three miles below, on the same river. He had gone to Sisterdale, a charming little valley where several distinguished German families have found an asylum. Two brooks, called the Sisters, unite their waters, and empty into the Guadaloupe on the north. First we passed the house of Mr. Dequer,[19] once Secretary of the Interior of the German Republic. We saw his lady, who seemed to regret that she could not talk English, as much as I that I could not talk German. His house is large, and built in a substantial manner. The males of the society, it seemed, were assembled at Mr. Dresler's, three miles up the dale.[20] It would be tedious to attempt to convey an idea of every pretty land-scape that one meets with in a country where there is so much that is beautiful. Yet there were two views that I had that day seen that will remain well-defined when all other impressions shall become confused and indistinct. Those were the crossing of the Guadaloupe, looking up stream, where there is a long reach of still water, with the two banks of the river walled in by those great cypress-trees stretching their branches across, as if they would unite; the other was a landscape, with a wall of dark blue limestone rising fifteen or twenty feet on the right, capped with shrubbery and with the softer strata washed out,

---

[18] The county seat of Comal County, New Braunfels, was founded in 1845 when Prince Carl of Solms-Braunfels settled a group of immigrants. Rudolf Leopold Biesele, *The History of the German Settlements in Texas,* pp. 120-21.

[19] Mr. Dequer probably is the "Mr. D." visited by Olmsted. See Olmsted, *Journey Through Texas,* pp. 196-97.

[20] The Comal County census of 1850 lists Julius, Rudolph, Jane, and Emile as members of the Dresel family. See Oscar Haas, *History of New Braunfels and Comal County, Texas, 1844-1846* (Austin: privately printed, 1968), p. 248.

leaving the rock very much in relief, with trees growing up at intervals to relieve, but not to conceal, the rock; from this, a flat stretching to the left, a noisy brook, and a lawn terminating in a thicket, and in front a bold, rocky promontory, with the house of Professor Kapp[21] half-concealed in the trees; and it was all just as it came from the hand of Nature. There was to be a musical festival at New Braunsfels, fifty miles distant, and preparations were making to attend it. It was decided that I should accompany the party—my horse was to be left to recover more perfectly from his injury, and I should ride one of theirs. Mr. Tyson and myself were to pass the night at Dresler's. This people lost their entire crops last year from drouth; and, having their means invested in lands, they have experienced a hard year, and enjoy but few of the luxuries of the table; they have but little time for hunting, and their horses are frequently stolen by Indians; but they bear all their privations with a cheerfulness that is truly exemplary, and social life is kept up in a manner such as is seen in few favored American communities. After our repast of corn-bread and milk, the evening was spent in the narrations of incidents of life on the frontiers. It was but natural that they whose ears had been deafened by the roar of revolutionary cannon, could fearlessly brave the dangers of the wilderness. I was told that, but a short time before, a panther had been very troublesome to the farm of Mr. Dequer, and had, in spite of all their efforts, destroyed much of their

---

21 Dr. Ernst Kapp was born in October 1808 in Germany. He received his Ph.D. at the University of Bonn in 1828 and taught at Hamm and Minden. He wrote several books and articles both before coming to Texas and after returning to Germany. He was imprisoned briefly in 1848 for advocating a more liberal German government. He moved to Sisterdale where he farmed and established a mineral water cure in 1849. In 1853 he was elected president of Der Freier Verein, a political organization of mostly German intellectuals. He returned to Germany for a visit in 1864 and decided to remain. He died in 1896. See Webb, Carroll, and Branda (eds.), *Handbook of Texas,* I, pp. 937-38; Geue and Geue (comps. & eds.), *A New Land Beckoned,* p. 110. See also Ethel Hander Geue (ed.), *New Homes in a New Land: German Immigration to Texas, 1847-1861* (Waco: Texian Press, 1970), p. 89.

stock; one night, in the absence of Mr. D., his dogs treed him, and two boys of about fourteen and sixteen, sons of Mr. D., accompanied by their mother, who held a light, shot him dead. It measured nine feet in length.[22]

It was midnight when we retired to the second floor to sleep. I looked out of a little porthole in the wall, just large enough to receive my head. The moon was shining full in a cloudless sky. My horse, which was staked out, contrary to our usual practice, was just discernible, and I heard him neigh from loneliness; felt some misgivings, and felt half-resolved to take a blanket and go stay by him. I listened to what further might be in the wind, but heard nothing else, save the chuck-wills-widow from a neighboring tree, and laid down and slept till late. I looked out in the morning to see how fared "Pelicano," but he was not there. I hurried down to learn what it meant, and found that all the horses on the place were gone.[23] This was a catastrophe to me so great that I could not contemplate it. I tried to find the trail by which they had left, but on the dry ground, to my unpractised eye, there was no trail. I went down to Mr. Dequer's, three miles distant. His dogs engaged the Indians in his yard, and he hastened out in his night dress, gun in hand—but they were too quick for him, though they did not succeed in getting any of his horses. The trail was found the next morning, and recognized as that of a Waco[24] who had visited them before. And there remained no doubt that my

---

[22] This story is also told in Olmsted, *Journey Through Texas,* p. 197.

[23] Even Stillman's friend, Douai, noted the loss of Pelicano in reporting the Indian raid. *San Antonio Zeitung,* June 2, 1855, p. 3, col. 3.

[24] The Waco Indians, a Wichita tribe, lived near present-day Waco, but roamed throughout West Texas. Lieutenant William H. C. Whiting encountered rumors of their depredations when he was probing the Trans-Pecos region in 1849. "Journal of William Henry Chase Whiting, 1849," in Ralph P. Bieber (ed.), *Exploring Southwestern Trails, 1846-1854* (Glendale: Arthur H. Clark Co., 1938), p. 249. Most of the tribe went to the Brazos Indian Reservation in 1855. Webb, Carroll, and Branda (eds.), *Handbook of Texas,* II, p. 848.

pet horse was in the hands of the savages, and I should never look upon his white face, and he should never neigh for me again. One can hardly realize, who has journeyed, as I had done, for weeks in a strange, wild land, with no other companion than his horse, with whom he had travelled by day and slept at night, how strong the attachment will become. He was as gentle and playful as a dog, and would follow me wherever he had an opportunity; when in lonely wild places he seemed to share my fears, and his instincts have often determined me. I had now brought him into the hands of those who would never respect his virtues or have compassion on him, but ride him without mercy on their marauding expeditions until he can go no longer, or until he is eaten. I felt it more keenly even than my own forsaken condition; and I was here with my journey half completed, without the ability to provide another horse, nor had we the means of pursuit, and perhaps it was as well that we had not, for there was, no doubt, a large party of them. The same day, about ten miles further down, a white man was killed and his horses taken— a negro accompanying him escaped. A consultation of war was held, when it was concluded that as we had neither the horses, nor one sufficiently skilled in trailing, we would go to the *song-verein*. A waggon [*sic*], with the balance of the animals left in the settlement, was soon in readiness, and my character as a gay cavalier was resigned for a seat in the bottom of the waggon. We were a company of eight including Mrs. Dequer; and, while they were singing the songs of their Fatherland, full of glee at the anticipated anniversary,[25] I was sad at the vicissitudes of fortune, and full of speculations as to my future course.

Truly yours,   J.D.B.S.

---

[25] The men were on their way to the Third German Texan Sängerfest in New Braunfels, which was held May 27-30, 1855. See *Neu-Braunfelser Zeitung*, Mar. 16, May 25, and June 8, 1855.

The Crayon (New York), II (July 25, 1855), pp. 49-50.

Wanderings in the Southwest
No. IV

San Antonio de Bexar, June 9th, 1855.

From Sisterdale to near Braunsfels [*sic*], a distance of fifty-two miles, the road leads over a hilly country. Within the first few hours we passed two pretty streams with grass valleys, in one of which was a cabin. As we passed, the company struck up a German song, when out rushed an occupant, in a degree of excitement, that told well how strong is the bond which holds them in sympathy in exile. I did not understand the words of the song, but I knew its meaning by its effect—it was a rallying call. He would have joined us, bare-headed as he was, but he had no money; one of the party arranged the matter by engaging a bundle of shingles, and paying in advance. He hastened to drive a calf into a pen near the house, to make it safe from the wolves, and on we drove. That night we camped in a valley without water, and as I laid my head upon the saddle, it pressed unusually heavy, and ached with the excitement of the day. We were in the valley of the dry Civolo, where that stream pursues its subterranean way, carrying with it all the springs that are necessary to make a mountain region an agreeable one to travel in. The coolness of the night breeze, as I lay on the ground with nothing over me but the starry sky, reduced the fever of my brain, and in part atoned for the want of those cool revulets, that in the mountain regions of the North sparkle by every man's door. There is a charm in the night air through all the inland regions of western Texas, that one can hardly appreciate who has not experienced it. When the sun goes down there is a softness in the breeze, (and one is scarcely ever without it) even when it is strong, that soothes the travel-worn into forgetfulness of his fatigues, and he sleeps as tranquilly and dreamless, and insensible to the hard earth, as the dead. Once I waked on hearing a horse grazing near my head; for an instant I forgot that Pelicano was a captive among the savages, and felt as a ranger, free to mount and away at my will. The moon was just resting on the summit of a distant mountain, my companions were sleeping around me on the grass, and the long Missouri wagon,[1] with its great shear, stood in the shadow of a post-oak. I would have given all this beautiful scene, the genial skies and smiling earth, for one draught of the cold water that at that moment blessed the least favored land of the North. We resumed our way early the next morning to get water, passing some charming valleys of great extent, with rich soil, covered with bright green grass, and interspersed with groves of oak, and intersected by the dry bed of the Civolo, but which is the bed of a torrent in the rainy season, and which is well defined by trees and vines that grow in greater profusion along its course. An artesian well would enable one to irrigate a thousand acres of the finest land in Texas. About ten o'clock we reached the house of a German settler. The water we used was drawn from a spring two or three miles distant, in a cask placed on a sled. We breakfasted on milk and eggs, of which we found here a good supply.

After an hour's rest, we continued our way over a road through a district entirely different from any that I had seen in Texas. Heretofore, all the country I had gone through, might be mistaken at a distance for one under a state of cultivation. I had seen nothing that could be called wild. The valley became hemmed in by mountains of limestone, covered by cedars, branching close to the ground, and spreading, making an impen-

---

[1] Missouri wagons were quite common in the West, particularly along the Santa Fe Trail. See Henry Pickering Walker, *The Wagonmasters, High Plains Freighting from the Earliest Days of the Santa Fé Trail to 1880* (Norman: Univ. of Okla. Press, 1966), p. 136.

etrable thicket. Bluffs of the same rock rise several hundred feet from the water-worn but dry ravine, above which eagles were hovering. It was a wilderness, where the bear, and panther, and rattlesnake reign undisturbed. We pass the high ridge dividing the valley of the Civolo from that of Comal creek,[2] also dry, and continued our way over arid and desolate hills, covered with prickly pears breast high, small oaks, and scanty grass. Three miles from New Braunsfels [*sic*] we had passed several cultivated fields, in which corn looked surprisingly well, and where the settlers supply themselves with water from wells. Here, on the top of the highest hill, overlooking the town and the extensive rolling prairie beyond, was a house intended as a resort from town. Here we stopped, and unrolled two banners, on one side of each was "Sisterdale," on the reverse of one was in German, "In the mountains is freedom," on the other the first line of a song, "What a dusty year it is." The hoops of the wagon—we had no cover—were wreathed with grape vines, evergreens, and scarlet flowers. The driver carried a vine over his shoulder, and we all wore a wreath of the same about our hats; I having had a horse stolen in their settlement, was thereby constituted a member of their society, and entitled to its privileges, and had a wreath of vines about my hat, while my sunburnt, unshaven face, would make me pass very well for one of them. Thus attired, we drove down the long hill past the Comal Springs,[3] and into the town singing a wine song, cheered by every group of a delighted and excited population. Mrs. D. was left at the house of a friend, and we drove through the town to the reception hall. Never till my dying day will I

---

2 Comal Creek, in south central Comal County, flows into the Comal River after traversing about four miles of territory. Webb, Carroll, and Branda (eds.), *Handbook of Texas,* I, p. 383.

3 Comal Springs flows from the limestone strata that make up the Balcones Escarpment in the northwestern part of New Braunfels. There the Comal River has its source. *Ibid.,* I, p. 383.

forget the scene that followed. It was the great anniversary, the re-union of friends, who have been tried together in the school of adversity. The republicans of '48,[4] who have suffered imprisonment, confiscation, and exile; the statesman, the poet, the philosopher, the artist, and naturalist, met after the conflicts of a year of toil and hardship, to sing once more the songs of the loved classic Rhine, to mingle with the aroma of its wine the cherished remembrances of home, which glows nowhere more vividly than in the heart of the German. How could I witness those congratulations, those beard-to-beard embraces of old friends, and not be moved; I, too, felt that I was a German, and not a member of the "Know Nothing"[5] inhospitable nation that I was. I shook hands with a hundred persons, not one of whom had I ever seen before. But Mr. Degner,[6] one of the most heroic spirits, and the most cheerful under adversity, that I ever knew, was not permitted to touch the ground; his friends bore him into the house with huzzas; we were all unceremoniously rushed into a room, and mixed in so much confusion, that I could scarcely distinguish myself from a German. A

---

[4] Many republicans fled Germany in 1848 after the liberals gained control of the government. The liberal-republican conflict was part of a general unrest that swept Europe in 1848. See Priscilla Robertson, *Revolutions of 1848, a Social History* (N.Y: Harper Torchbook, 1960), pp. 147-49.

[5] The Know-Nothings, or the American Party, organized around a platform of Americanism, including biases against aliens and Catholics, hence were unfriendly to the Germans of South Central Texas. They included such famous Texans as Sam Houston and John S. ("Rip") Ford in the mid-1850s. John S. Ford, *Rip Ford's Texas,* ed. by Stephen B. Oates (Austin: Univ. of Tex. Press, 1963), p. xxx.

[6] Edward Degener (or Deginer), born in Brunswick, Germany, in 1809, served in the Anhalt-Dessay legislature and was a member of the first National Assembly at Frankfort in 1848. He immigrated to Texas in 1850 and settled at Sisterdale, where he farmed. A Unionist, he was court-martialed and imprisoned during the Civil War. He served in the Texas Constitutional conventions of 1866 and 1868-1869, and upon readmission of Texas to the Union, was elected Republican representative to the Forty-first Congress in 1870-1871. He was a member of the San Antonio City Council from 1872-1878, and died in 1890. Webb, Carroll, and Branda (eds.), *Handbook of Texas,* I, p. 482; Geue and Geue (comps. and eds.), *New Land Beckoned,* p. 88; Carpenter (ed.) *Texas Federal Population Schedule,* II, p. 571; Geue (ed.), *New Homes,* p. 62.

table loaded with refreshments, moved me still deeper, while
one of their number sat upon the floor astride a beer cask, and
filled the glasses as fast as they were emptied. Hungry and
thirsty as we were, would not you have done as we did. I forgot my nationality, and if I had not broken away, I should
soon have been able to talk German, although I did not get so
far as to understand a word of it. Festivities were kept up till
a late hour of the night, though not having the elasticity of
constitution that enables me to resist the fatigues of a long
day's ride under a burning sun, seated on a box in the bottom
of a wagon, I took an early opportunity to retire. Judge Behr,
on his way to Europe, and myself, were entertained at the
house of a gentleman, whose wife was a highly cultivated lady
but recently arrived; she spoke English very fluently, and their
house was made my home during my stay. Their refined and
generous hospitality will not soon be forgotten. It is but nine
years since this colony was formed and deserted by the speculators, who had taken all their money, leaving them in a
state of starvation and suffering, from which many perished,
and at this moment they have a city, where there is more
industry and comfort, and even luxury, than can be found in
any place which I have visited in Western Texas. One of the
many subterranean rivers of Texas bursts out about a mile
above the town called Comal Springs, and unites itself with
the Guadaloupe just below. In the afternoon of the next day, a
procession was formed of the various singing societies forming
the association, each with its banner, and preceded by a band
of music, it marched out of town about a mile distant, to a hall
built of stone expressly for the occasion, two hundred feet long,
on the high bluff bank of the river.[7] During the evening the
hall was crowded, while each society took the stage in turn.
After this was a collation, at which the whole company sat
down, and about twelve o'clock, all but a few loiterers were

gone. Three days were given to the festivities. The second evening was devoted to a ball in the same place, the third to theatricals. The daytime was spent in social entertainment at private houses, and if I, a stranger, could be permitted to judge, by my own experience, there was much enjoyment.

Setting aside, if possible, for a short time the conceit that we are the greatest nation alive; that we have reached the highest attainment of moral and social development possible; that our political institutions do not admit of improvement; that for anything to be American is to be an example to all people for ever, there might be found much in the social life of the Germans to be imitated, which would soften our national austerity, that painful effort to be *respectable,* and teach us how to make use of the means in our hands to make ourselves and others happy. We are charged with being an avaricious people, who make it the chief object of life to get wealth, without knowing how to make use of it. If our social natures were better developed, it would effect a cure. Men persevere in getting rich, because they do not find enjoyment in any other way. They do not know how to be happy. Music with the German is the great smelting agent that softens all their cares, and fuses all classes into one democratic mass, and elevates them into a higher and purer life. Were they to abandon their "lager bier," the change would not be perceptible in that respect. We are accounted a democratic people, yet are we not ever on the watch to check any unwarrantable encroachments upon our dignity? We encircle ourselves in a halo of caste, and repel

[7] Stillman attended the third German Texan Sängerfest, which was held on May 27-30, 1855, at the new sangerhalle, which had just been completed. *Neu-Braunfelser Zeitung,* Mar. 16, p. 2, col. 4; May 25, p. 2, col. 6; June 8, 1855, p. 2, col. 3; p. 3, col. 4; and p. 4, col. 1; *The Galveston Weekly News,* May 29, 1855, p. 2, col. 1. The new sangerhalle is shown in a Julius Ploetz painting, illustrated in Cecelia Steinfeldt, *Texas Folk Art: One Hundred Fifty Years of the Southwestern Tradition* (Austin: Tex. Monthly Press, 1981), pp. 42, 44.

every one who approaches us without the proper credentials. This state of things will perhaps continue while we have menial classes amongst as [us]; but while it does exist, we might find much to imitate in the German democrat. I have seen a world-renowned naturalist, an honorary member of European societies; a jurist from the highest judicial tribunal in his native land; a professor of her university; a priest from her altars; a secretary of the interior in the republic; the son of the prime minister of the crown; some as poor as the poorest, and others in possession of great wealth, all seated at one table with the peasant, and from their demeanor you could not tell the peasant from the prince—all melted and bowed before the majesty of song. There, too, was a professor music, the composer of several operas, his hand hardened and browned by toil; an aged Anchises,[8] who[se] heroic son had borne him from a patriot's prison, and was sharing with him his exile. Yet they were in an ale-house, each with his mug of beer. There were no low songs or vulgar stories, the usual accompaniment of the convivial gatherings of our most cultivated classes, when the ladies are absent. I saw no quarrelling or discourtesy. You may say that I have not an American heart. I have been frequently told that I was a foreigner.

Having an opportunity to return to this place on the second day of these festivities, I took a hurried leave of New Braunfels. Having a sick horse to travel with, we made but slow progress, and did not reach town until four o'clock in the morning, encountering one of those severe thunderstorms to which this country is liable. The wind and lightning were violent, tearing away all our shelter, and drenching us in rain.

J.D.B.S.

---

[8] Anchises, in Greek mythology, was the father of Aeneas, who was the defender of Troy and the hero of the *Aeneid* by Virgil.

The Crayon (New York), II (August 1, 1855), pp. 65-67.

Wanderings in the Southwest
No. V

San Antonio de Bexar, June 11th, 1855.

Two elements which enter into the topography of Western Texas will give the key to the physical geography.[1] There are, firstly, the cretaceous formation, which prevails over all those parts that I have visited, and, secondly, the excessive rains to which it is subject at certain seasons of the year. All the rock that I have seen, and I am told that there is no other until you reach the interior regions drained by the waters of the upper Colorado,[2] where the primary formations abound, corresponds in all respects to the formation of the Paris basin. All the fossils which I have found are represented in that formation, though of differing species. Among these are ammonites, several species of Exogyra, nautilus, &c. The hills are all of limestone, covered in most places with a thick coat of detritus and siloceous stones intermixed with fossil shells.

This rock so closely resembles the French Caen stone of which the public buildings of Paris, and Westminster Abbey are built, and which has recently been imported into New York, that if I were to place a fragment of each before you, you would be at a loss to decide which came from Texas and which came from France. It is unquestionably the best building material in use, so soft, that when quarried it may be cut with an

---

[1]Ferdinand Roemer was the first modern geologist to study the region that Stillman visited. See Walter Keene Ferguson, *Geology and Politics in Frontier Texas, 1845-1909* (Austin: Univ. of Tex. Press, 1969), pp. 51-52. For Roemer's account, see Ferdinand Roemer, *Texas with Particular Reference to German Immigration and the Physical Appearance of the Country,* trans. by Oswald Mueller (San Antonio: Standard Printing Co., 1935) and *Die Kreidebildungen von Texas und ihre organisehen, Einsehlüsse* (Bonn: Adolph Marcus, 1852).

[2] The Colorado River flows some 600 miles through Texas, rising in northeastern Dawson County in West Texas, and flowing through Matagorda County into Matagorda Bay. Webb, Carroll, and Branda (eds.), *Handbook of Texas,* I, p. 379.

axe, or split into slabs with a saw, and hardening by exposure to the air. Whether it will bear the exposure to the severe frost of the North is a question which the people of New York will, no doubt, have an opportunity to determine. Its strata I have not found disturbed by igneous forces, and the softness and porosity of some of them has given rise to some very curious phenomena. At Leona Springs,[3] sixty miles from Eagle Pass,[4] on the Rio Grande, a subterranean river breaks out just where the mountain region ends and the alluvial begins; four miles above this place, the San Antonio takes its rise in the same manner, not in one volume as has been represented, but in the immediate vicinity and apparently from nearly the same stratum, swelling in the distance of a quarter of a mile into a stream not sensibly augmented by all the streams that flow into it, at this time of drouth, above the junction of the Medina. It is a clear, sparkling, rapid, but noiseless stream, filling its channel full, suffering no change with the vicissitudes of moisture or temperature, to which the country is subject. Pecans, the loftiest and most beautiful tree on the plains, throw their shades over it. The loaded vines of the mustang grape drop their cluster into its waters, while ferns clothe its margin in the richest green. One of these springs is worth a long journey to see. It is a well ten or twelve feet deep, running over full of water of the very standard of purity. As you lean against the tree that declines over it and look down into it, you could not tell but for a slight ripple on its surface where the atmosphere ends and water begins. A plant with a small peltate leaf of bright green lines the rock down to the bottom, and is scattered over the

---

[3] Stillman probably is referring to the Leona River, which rises in Uvalde County and flows into the Frio River in southern Frio County, rather than Leona Creek, which is located in Victoria County. *Ibid.,* II, p. 49.

[4] Founded in 1849, Eagle Pass, the county seat of Maverick County, was established by the army because of the need for a temporary base in the region. *Ibid.,* I, p. 532.

View of "Neu-Braunfels. Deutsche Colonie in West Texas"

Made after a sketch by Carl G. von Iwonski, from the Vereinsberg, a hill south of the village, about the time of Stillman's visit.

Courtesy of Eugene C. Barker Texas History Center, University of Texas, Austin

The Saengerhalle (singing hall), right, was new when Stillman visited
Probably painted by Julius Ploetz within five years of Stillman's visit. It stood next to
Hermann Seele's log cabin (center).
Courtesy of Sophienburg Memorial Association, New Braunfels

white sandy floor, and each is in constant vibration as the water rises past them. The temperature, like that of all those springs of which I could get any reliable information, is a little higher than the mean atmospheric temperature of the year. This is an exception to Humboldt's rule,[5] that in all hot climates the average temperature of the springs is lower. The temperature of the springs here is 74° and does not vary much from that during the year; however, I am inclined to believe that a careful record has not been kept. I only know positively that the temperature now is as I have stated. At New Braunsfels is another river, starting one mile from town, and flowing past it with a volume equal to that of the San Antonio, but its channel receives the drainage of a considerable region above during the rainy season, and is therefore, shut in by high alluvial banks. At San Marcos,[6] east of the Colorado, is said to be still another of these famous springs. I have spoken in a previous letter of the sudden disappearance of the Civolo about thirty miles north of this. From that place there is a dry channel for a distance of forty miles, when water again appears in the form of springs, making a stream of half the size of the Civolo where its waters sink in the limestone rock. There seems to be no reasonable ground of belief that the streams are identical, for the circumstances that determine the course of a river on the surface of the earth, cannot be supposed to control its subterranean channel. I am more inclined to believe that the upper Civolo, after its disappearance, being augmented by the drainage of the region under which it flows, finds its exit at the

---

[5] Alexander von Humboldt was a well-known German naturalist who traveled widely in, and wrote authoritatively about, the New World. See Douglas Botting, *Humboldt and the Cosmos* (N. Y: Harper & Row, 1973).

[6] Located in Hays County, San Marcos was inspected by José Joaquín de Eca y Músquiz in 1750, and was the site of the San Xavier Mission in 1755. The Anglo-Americans began settling there in 1847. The springs of the San Marcos River now are a famous tourist attraction. Webb, Carroll, and Branda (eds.), *Handbook of Texas*, II, pp. 558-59.

Comal Springs, many miles nearer. In the excursion which I
shall make this week to the Leona and the Nueces,[7] I may be
able to add something to this subject. The geological division
of the region I have travelled over should be made by a line
drawn through this belt of springs, that above being limestone,
and that below, with some exceptions, being alluvial, that distinction being not so apparent as might be supposed, did we not
take into account the soft and perishable nature of the rock, and
the force of heavy floods. The hills below the springs are chiefly
of an alluvium of chalk, containing recent shells, of species
now living. It is used for building purposes, but is so soft and
friable as scarcely to admit handling, nor does it become hard
by exposure. Near Helena, this white alluvium appears, but
lower down. There is, strickly speaking, but little prairie land
in Western Texas, as might be inferred from what I have said
already. The elevation, though almost imperceptible, is uniform
from the sea coast to this place, which has an elevation of six
hundred feet. The rivers all have a uniform current from the
limestone region to the sea. The country intersected by them
is, near the sea, generally level, but ravines begin to show
themselves before you have travelled five miles; these increase
in size as you penetrate the country; and the surface becomes
rolling, or hilly even, to people whose ideas have been formed
in a level country. These are the general features, modified, of
course, by local causes of no general interest. I cannot avoid
observing, in passing, the great contrast that obtains between
Texas and California, in respect to this physical feature. In all
these points the alluvial districts of the latter country are directly the reverse. The Sacramento,[8] or its tributaries, receive no

---

[7] Rising in Edwards County, the Nueces River flows through Uvalde, Zavala, Dim-
met, LaSalle, McMullen, and Live Oak counties and forms the boundary between
Jim Wells and San Patricio and Nueces counties before pouring into Nueces Bay.
Ibid., II, p. 291.

[8] In California.

accession from the plains, but, on the contrary, the water flows from the river on the plains; the land is highest on the bank of the river. It would be interesting to trace the difference further, even into the vegetation, as in the preponderance of the grasses over the flowering plants in Texas; the almost entire usurpation of the latter in California: but I am writing of Texas. One that has travelled through Texas need not be told that it is subject to periods of excessive rains—the whole features of the country, ancient and recent, betray the fact: but the drainage of the country is so good that, though there are but few bridges or ferries, communication through the country is said to be not long suspended. During the summer there is less rain falls than in the north—not sufficient to affect the streams to any great degree. During the last month there have been three thunder-storms passing over this place coming from the northwest; the last was followed by a light north wind for three days—during the rest of the time a breeze has been blowing from the southeast, by day and by night; this, taken in connection with the dryness of the atmosphere, which is remarkable, have the effect to make the climate comfortable in the shade, during the hottest weather. This breeze is generally so strong, as to blow papers across the room; but to say that the sun does not do his work well, would be doing him great injustice.

The thermometer generally stands, at noon, in the shade, on the north side of the house at 90°, yet the starch in my collar— we do wear collars here—would not be softened, a catastrophe that would be sure to take place in New York with a temperature of 80° in the coldest place I could find. Laborers work all day in the sun, yet I never heard a case of *coup de soleil,* cause why, the evaporation from their bodies keeps the temperature of them down, and they don't "melt their kidneys." As an artist, you will say that the atmosphere is *"cold,"* the sky is intensely blue, the green on the most distant hill is, at this season—understand I only speak positively of what I know —as green as that in the neighboring garden, the sun shows fight to the last, and wherever his latest beam falls upon you, it feels like the concentrated focus of a sun-glass; he goes not down with a "battle-stained eye." You see, therefore, there is no chance for the melo-dramatic effect of your hot-house landscape painters. No dew falls at night; though the nights are not warm, one may sleep on the ground with impunity, as many do habitually, at this season, as I have done often, and as I intend to do for the next two weeks, in a country where there has no white man settled. Perhaps, I may get back my beloved pony. We shall go, half a dozen of us, well armed, and, perhaps the Indians will try to steal some more horses! Having no marshes, there are no mosquitos; or, at least, so few as scarcely to be represented in the entomology of this vicinity: they are said to be extremely troublesome nearer the coast. I have not observed the fly that is so troublesome to horses in high latitudes, and they have not, therefore, the habit of stamping the ground: there is a large green fly here that stings them, but they are rare. Per contra, there is an insect here abounding through the early part of the year, but disappearing about the middle of summer; they pervade all places, and are most abundant where they are most to be expected, but when you put your finger on them they ain't there; a genus, with nocturnal habits, that may be cultivated in beds adapted to them, with but little attention. The only order of insects that abound here in great variety are the coleoptera or beetle family; it is too dry for butterflies. Of the orthoptera there are some fine representatives, one of which is the mantis, whose fabulous character has made it an object of superstition among all people where it is found. Lindheimer,[9] the botanist, told me, at New Braunsfels, that he had domesticated one to catch flies about his home, in which it was very useful, and lived with him a long time.

There is, also, found here a phasmidae, a stick with six legs, and nearly as many inches long, one of the largest of the whole insect class.

I have taken much pains to ascertain what may be done here in the cultivation of fruit. It is apparent from what I have already written that the characteristics of this climate, are those of the temperate rather than the torrid region. Under the Mexican population no attempt was made to cultivate what required much care; and the white emigration has been too recent to permit them to devote much time to the luxuries of life. I have been told by those who have been long in the country, that the ants would destroy fruit trees by stripping them of their leaves, and that there was no way of destroying them. At this place I find several gentlemen who have turned their attention to that branch of horticulture. Mr. Lewis and Mr. Vance have both fine gardens. They have succeeded in destroying the ants —one, by digging; the other, by poisoning with arsenic. The latter mode is the cheapest and most effectual. Mr. Vance mixed arsenic and corn-meal, and placed it near their nests daily, until there is not to be found one upon his premises. In his grounds, which are irrigated with a well this year for the first time, he had peaches, plums, apples, pomegranates, figs, cherries, apricots and grapes, all thriving well. Figs are abundant all along the river, where they have survived the decline of industry in places now otherwise waste places. Pomegranates need no attention; the El Paso grape needs but little care, and is the finest grape in the country. I saw a cluster in Mr. Vance's garden, on which I counted over three hundred grapes, and it makes the finest wine. Mr. Lewis has not irrigated, and he has found no

---

9 Ferdinand Leindheimer (Lindheimer), the botanist, probably was the same man Olmsted visited. He immigrated in 1839. He had lived a short time in Wisconsin before coming to Texas. He edited and published the *Neu-Braunfelser Zeitung*. See Olmsted, *Journey Through Texas*, pp., 169-71, 178; Geue and Geue (comps.), *New Land Beckoned*, p. 120; Geue (ed.), *New Homes*, p. 27.

difficulty with any of the above-mentioned fruits. He raises an abundance of peaches, and his apple-trees, though small, have this year several bushels growing upon them, and he says their flavor is equal to any that are raised at the North; his trees, however, were sent from the North, and I suspect that the character of a fruit will degenerate by an acclimation. The apple thrives well in Peru, South America, but its flavor is lost. The banana succeeds well on the coast, but here it has not been tried; it requires a humid climate. There are orange-trees growing, but not old enough to prove their capability to bear. The drouth of the present season, unprecedented in the experience of the fruit-growers, will prove a severe test of those trees, not irrigated. That this region of Texas is not subject to frost is a fable; it was so severe last winter as to kill all the fig-trees that I have seen, except those in that town; and its severity here was abated by the temperature of the San Antonio river, which is said never to be lower at this place than 70°. Shoots are springing up again with great vigor from the roots. The Mustang grape grows in the greatest abundance along all the streams, and is the only indigenous fruit of any great value. It is very large; one that I measured this week, as an average sized grape, was two and a half inches in circumference, and I am told that they have not yet attained their full growth. One could make the finest jelly, at no cost, except for the sugar. There is a species of plum growing wild along the water-courses, said to be very delicious, but the fruit was cut off this season by the late frosts. Many years since, under the rule of the missions, thousands of acres, extending over a region eight miles long and from two to four wide, were under high cultivation; the ditches that were dug will remain, and venerable pecans growing upon their banks attest to their antiquity, but the fields which they irrigated are now waste. A few recent inclosures by Germans and Americans are cultivated, and, by deeper plowing, they find irrigation not so necessary, for most purposes, as was supposed by the Mexicans.

The monuments which those old Spanish missionaries have left on the San Antonio furnish the chief object of interest to passing strangers, and their history carries us back to a time coeval with the settlement of some of our Old Thirteen. One is astonished at their enterprise, and the magnitude of their labors, not only in cultivation of a wilderness surrounded by the most formidable savages on the continent, but the edifices they built, elegant even now in their ruins. The style of these edifices is that so common through all the old Spanish colonies —they are massive and rudely elegant. Within a distance of nine miles, there are three of these mission buildings.[10] A ride from town down the bank of the river in the shade of the pecan trees to the first one forms a favorite excursion in the afternoon, and to those who have not seen a fine ruin before, it rewards them well. As you approach it, the dome and towers will appear entire above the rich green of the trees, and gilded by the setting sun. I rode my horse through the door of the church and stood under the dome still retaining the painted fresco devices. The corners of the arch of the transept were completely occupied by bats; indeed, the whole place was but a hive of them, and if Proserpine[11] had held her court there, they could not have been more numerous. It was just about the time that they issue forth, and some stones thrown into their dense masses awakened them from the torpor of the day, and they swarmed out in myriads, keeping an unbroken column until they had well cleared the ruin, and then it was every bat for himself, and wo [*sic*] to every insect that was found on the

---

10 The three missions nine miles from San Antonio that Stillman mentions probably are San José y San Miguel de Aguayo, San Francisco de la Espada, and San Juan Capistrano. Webb, Carroll, and Branda (eds), *Handbook of Texas*, II, pp. 551, 556-57.

11 Proserpine (or Proserpina), a Greek goddess, daughter of Zeus and the earth-goddess Demeter, Queen of the Underworld, was worshipped in Rome.

wing. When we left the place, the stream of bats still continued unabated. The ride down the bank of the river furnishes some very picturesque scenery, unlike anything I have seen elsewhere; not extensive, but perfect bijoux for an artist. The Mexican character of this city is fast disappearing under the superior enterprise and taste of its new inhabitants, but much of the old order still remains. The church of the Alamo, now used for government stores, still stands with its battle-scarred walls, where Crocket [*sic*] and his companions fell. I think there is no place in America that has been the theater of more desperate fights, even from the earliest times, and no place is more fruitful of the material of romance than this place, but its history is unwritten, and the few who remain of those who participated in the most modern of its legends are fast passing away.[12] The plaza has still many of the one story adobe buildings, more like a wall, with windows and doors alternately, which were witnesses of the incursions of the Camanches [*sic*]; these still stand, and a gamecock tied to the door-post tells that a descendant of the founders of the colony there keeps a store. The bell of the church daily rings its matin and vesper chimes, as it rung them nearly two centuries ago; but there has risen by their side the well-built stores of the invader which overtops them, where the auctioneer is knocking down goods at "immense sacrifice," and along the river are little villas that are fast rivalling those of Italy. When I first rode into town, I felt something of disappointment—I knew it was a frontier town which, in 1850, had but 3,000 inhabitants, and the Mexican hovels, the multitude of dogs and half naked children that inhabited them, combined with a feeling of loneliness—that I was a stranger nearly 2,000 miles from any friend, depressed

---

12 The first serious history of Texas, Henderson Yoakum's *History of Texas From Its First Settlement in 1685 to Its Annexation to the United States in 1846,* appeared in 1855, but it probably was not distributed rapidly enough for Stillman to have seen a copy before writing this letter. See Jenkins, *Basic Texas Books,* pp. 590-93.

me. But when I looked about the country stretching away in every direction for hundreds of miles, of which this must be the commercial centre, became acquainted with the great number of enterprising northern men and indomitable Germans that have settled here, swelling her population in five years to 10,000; the peculiar advantages of this river head, winding about the place and passing everybody's door-yard; the delicious climate, that combines the mildness of the South with the healthfulness of the North, I felt a regret that I must leave it, and could not occupy one of the many beautiful little nooks on the river bank, where I might permit my life to flow as pure and tranquilly as its waters. But I am in a reverie. I would recommend to builders and carpenters to direct their attention to this place. Good workmen will command two dollars and fifty cents a day, and three dollars, but to New York builders who will come out here with the capital to buy lots, and build to sell again, there is an easy fortune. The wood-work should be made at the North and sent to Port Lavaca, thence it is transported by Mexican ox-teams. It is only necessary for me to state the fact, that so great is the rage for investment in live stock and land, that money commands five per cent. a month on the best securities; rents are very high, because there are so many better ways of investing money than in building houses to let, even at such high rents. There is a stir and vigorous life here that I have seen in no inland city of the old states.

J.D.B.S.

The Crayon (New York), II (September 19, 1855), pp. 175-77.

Wanderings in the Southwest
No. VI

San Antonio de Bexar, July 16, 1855.

Our arrangements being completed for a journey of three weeks, through the unsettled region lying between this place and the Rio Grande, we appointed our rendezvous at a ranch on the Medina, about twelve miles from here. The party consisted of six persons, a judge, and his son, Sandy, one of the eight survivors of Hays' famous Rangers,[1] and two Mexicans, Antonio and Sechio. The judge provided himself with a two-horse carriage, to carry himself and our stores as far as a carriage could be driven, when he would ride one horse, and pack the other with the necessary stores and camp utensils. I was to find a horse at the ranch, and rode there with the judge. He was in the best of humor, and entertained me with much that was interesting in relation to the lands and his experiences in Texas. The road was in excellent condition though the rolling lands through which it led were brown from the long drouth. The quails were just leading out their young from the clumps of mesquet [*sic*] bushes, but besides these we saw no game; the country between the San Antonio and the Medina is so much ridden over in search of a stray cattle as to drive it farther back; a black wolf only crossed our track as we approached the river. The house was a low thatched cottage, built on a terrace, with the thickly wooded ravine in front, through which the river flowed far below, and a ledge of sandstone in the rear. Sechio was sent to get such horses as were required, and to stake them

---

1 John Coffee Hays commanded a band of Texas Rangers, who acted as scouts for the U. S. Army during the Mexican War. See James K. Greer, *Colonel Jack Hays: Texas Frontier Leader and California Builder* (N.Y: E. P. Dutton, 1952).

out so as to have them in readiness for the morning. Here we learned that the night before all the horses from the neighboring settlements above had been carried off by the Indians, that a party of five men, badly armed, and worse mounted, had gone in pursuit and overtaken the Indians, three in number, preparing their breakfast. Instead of charging upon them at once, the only successful mode of fighting them, they delivered their fire at a distance, during which the red skins mounted their best horses and escaped. The white men then returned for reinforcements, and a party of twenty had gone in pursuit. Sechio saw three the same day on foot in the immediate vicinity of the ranch. As a precaution, the horses we were to use on the morrow were staked out late in the evening, in a secluded place, and the *caballada* of about fifty horses and mules turned out late into the thickets of mesquet, so that if the Indians had been prowling about they would not find them where they expected. The company were soon scattered about upon skins and blankets for the night, and I chose my bed under the shelter of a wide spreading live oak above the terrace where the waggon was left. About midnight Sandy arrived with letters for me from home, for which he had waited until the arrival of the mail. I perused them by the flickering flame of a tallow candle, and returned to my blanket, but not to sleep. My thoughts were on the wing, keeping company with the owls. I arose at daybreak and walked through the sleepers. All, even the dogs, were wrapped in that deep sleep of the dawn, which was always the favorite time of savage attack. The sky was overcast with grey clouds, as is usual in this region in summer, until they are scattered by the increasing heat of the sun. I strolled out to the place where we had picketed our horses, to be sure that they were quite secure, then down to the river to bathe. The interval before breakfast was occupied in preparing our arms. The Judge had a heavy double-barrelled gun, his son a "six shooter," Sandy a rifle and "six shooter," Antonio only an old dragoon pistol, and Sechio a much ridiculed flint-lock rifle. In cleaning Sandy's rifle the cone was broken, and the nearest place at which it could be repaired was Castroville; its place could not be supplied, and it was necessary to send it to that place. Judge jr. was sent with Antonio to get it repaired, and we appointed the "Cuacan Water Hole,"[2] seventeen miles distant, as the next rendezvous.

At breakfast we were startled by the report of a gun at the door; having heard a wrangling before breakfast among the Mexicans on account of a knife, we were at no loss to divine the meaning of the report. Sechio had, in a passion, fired my fowlingpiece, which happened to be loaded with fine bird-shot, at his antagonist, who had sought shelter behind a tent, and the shot were spent on the canvass [*sic*]. Sechio is decidedly a character; in his childhood he was taken prisoner in Mexico by the Camanches, during one of their forays into that coun-try, with a man who was liberated after having his nose cut off. He remained among them until Taylor's invasion of Mex-ico,[3] when a party of Americans made an attack upon the camp of Camanches where Sechio was held. In his effort to escape he was shot through the arm, being mistaken for an Indian, but he plead that he was a Christian, and for that time it saved his life, whether the same plea will save his soul, "Quien sabe?" as he would say in his language. Sandy found in Mexico a peon, with a debt of eighteen dollars, which was consigning him to slavery for life, and being pleased with his energy and daring bought his liberty and brought him with him to Texas. He is still young, very short and square-built, with strongly-marked Indian features.

---

2 Cuacan Water Hole cannot be identified.

3 General Zachary Taylor invaded Mexico from Texas in 1846, in the opening days of the U. S. war with Mexico.

A *vaquero,* who had been sent out to gather the horses return-ed with but two mules, and it was two o'clock before the lost animals were found, and we were ready to start. Our road led up the Medina on the left bank, but before we had gone five miles, it was discovered that my horse was lame, and Sechio was sent back with him to the ranch to supply his place, and meet us at the appointed rendezvous, while I rode his mule. "Sandy," said I, "that seems hard to send that boy on such an errand so late in the day, and to meet us at such an indefinable place as a 'water hole;' he will never be able to find us." "Trust him for that, his instincts are as keen as a bee's; you can't lose him. He will not follow our trail, but will strike a line for the camp, and will be there as soon as we." I did not like my mule; I never did like the abnormal race, and this one was Sechio's favorite, and the attachment seemed to be mutual, but between us there was no love lost. There was one particular gait that suited her, but to which I had a special aversion. When I spur-red her to take a gait that suited me better, she would send me too far ahead of my party, and if I checked her, she would drop back into a snail's pace, and put me far behind. I was forced to give her her way, at which she would drop back her long ears and switch her tail with delight, while she said in deeds more efficient than words, "Old Greenhorn, I'll give you some — you don't come it over me as you do over the short-eared kind." I found there was but little to be gained by quarrelling with a mule.

The country on the Medina is in high repute for its fertility, although it is not uniform in that respect. The best land is said to be that where the Mesquet and Hackberry or wild China trees abound. The country, abounding with the various species of oak found here, has a lighter and more sandy soil, but is remarkably picturesque. Sometimes, solitary oaks of large size, throwing their branches out so far and low that they rest upon the ground, their ends buried beneath it—at other times they grow small and many crowded together, where cattle may gather in an extended and unbroken shade. We followed up the Medina to the point where the old Presidio road crosses, and this was to be our guide as far as the Leona river.

From the Medina to the Chaean Creek,[4] a distance of about six miles, the country is hilly, of light sandy soil, sometimes flinty and scattered over with oaks, and, in some places, shrubs. About sundown we reached the Chaean, a creek when it rains violently, but, at other times, furnishes occasional "water holes." This one is known, par excellence, by that name, because it is the only one in the valley, for many miles, that does not become dry at some seasons. Here we unsaddled and turned our horses out into a fine growth of Mesquet grass, under the care of Sechio, who came upon the spot almost at the same time with us. Antonio soon had a fire; and coffee making, corn cake steaming under a heap of coals, and bacon, that *sine qua non* of a woods-man's camp fire, and, as an article of diet, the worst that a white man ever invented, was hissing and snapping in a pan. There you have now a peep into our fare. If we have any better, we must depend on our guns and fishing tackle; and he ought to congratulate himself who can always, in the wilderness, get enough of so simple fare as that. But, we did have here an unexpected luxury. A young man had a small stock of cattle in the vicinity, and his log cabin was hard by— and, upon his invitation, we helped ourselves to a plentiful supply of milk.

I was anxious to get a specimen of a chuck-wills-widow, and I heard one in a tree so close to me that I thought I should be able to shoot it, dark as it had become, but the sound kept at the same apparent distance from me, and led me into a thicket

---

4 Chaean Creek flowed from what is today Medina County into the Rio San Miguel, a tributary of the Rio Frio. See *Johnson's New Map.*

that grew at the head of the pond, and then I heard it off in another direction. All my efforts have, as yet, been ineffectual in securing that interesting bird. He is universally called here after the name of his northern congener, the whip-poor-will, though no articulation could be more distinct than that with which it pronounces its own name. Its sweet note is heard all night long in the thickets along every water-course, where it is concealed by day so as to be rarely seen. He who has once heard its song, while he lies wrapped in his blanket under the silent moon, and starts plowing the clouds, will feel its witchery awakening memories that would have slumbered, and leaving an impression that he will retain when the fatigues of travel, the hard ground on which he slept, and the harder bread and bacon on which he fed, shall be forgotten. I sometimes hear the mocking-bird by night, but in lonely thickets near the water, the chuck-wills-widow always. But, singing-birds, nor even "wills-widow" herself, could keep way-weary travellers from sleeping.

We started early the next morning, and rode over a hilly country mostly fertile, with post oak in abundance, and good grazing for cattle or sheep everywhere. The valley of the Black Creek[5] is especially a beautiful wide flat with rich, dark loam, with a heavy growth of grass, but the creek was wanting. The hills are sandy, and more or less covered with chapparel [*sic*] as we approach the Hondo;[6] and such is the favorite region of the rattle-snake—they are numerous between the Medina and the Rio Grande. This morning one sounded the alarm, just in front of our horses, and coiled himself in a clump of thorny bushes. It was the first I had seen in Texas—and, having fired

[5] There are several streams named Black Creek in Texas, but Stillman referred probably to the one that rises in Medina County and flows across Frio County into San Miguel Creek. Webb, Carroll, and Branda (eds.), *Handbook of Texas*, I, p. 169.

[6] Stillman probably is referring to Hondo Creek, which rises in southern Bandera County, flows through Medina County, and joins the Frio in Frio County. *Ibid.*, I, p. 831.

Military Plaza—San Antonio, Texas, by artist Arthur Schott

Schott was with the U.S. Boundary Survey in the early 1850s and this appeared as the frontispiece in William H. Emory's *United States and Mexican Boundary Survey.*

Courtesy of Amon Carter Museum, Fort Worth, Texas

View in Texas about 65 Miles North of San Antonio, c. 1849
Stillman traversed country similar to this depicted by artist Seth Eastman.
Courtesy of San Antonio Museum Association

both barrels of my gun, I cautiously approached to haul him from his covert with a long stick, but there was nothing to fear, I had shot his head off, and, taking his rattles as a trophy, we rode on. The common rattle-snake, though it attains as large size as in any part of the United States, is slow in its movements, and indisposed to act the offensive; they will escape without doing you harm, if you will give them an opportunity. I soon lost all fear of them, and would kill them with a small stick. My horse had a perfect horror of them, and had evidently been bitten by one; a crooked stick thrown down before her, or the noise of a rattle, would make it dangerous to an incautious rider. There is much popular misapprehension in regard to the effects of the bite of the rattle-snake, and hence of empyricism [*sic*] in its treatment. It is a common thing for dogs and other domestic animals to be bitten by them, but it is rarely that their bite is fatal. I know one dog that has been bitten several times, for he would attack them on every occasion; he received no treatment, but has become fearful of a snake. A Mexican was bitten during our absence, while sleeping on a cart at the ranch of Judge J. The reptile had crawled upon the cart to find a chicken, and, without doubt, the Mexican threw his hand over him. He was bitten in one finger. When we returned, his finger was a little swollen, but no constitutional effects followed the bite. I cannot say the same for the remedy, for the man was made drunk with whiskey; stimulants, such as the carbonate of ammonia, or whiskey, are no doubt useful just in counteracting the depressing influence of the poison, but I am very doubtful whether as many individuals do not recover without treatment as with it—and I am quite certain that when used to the extent of intoxication, it only co-operates with the poison in depressing the vital energies. Those cases of death from the bite of the rattlesnake, that have come to my knowledge, have been sudden; the poison had probably been

injected in a vein, and carried directly to the center of circulation, and so through all the system, and in such cases the best
treatment does not avail. Such a case occurred some years since
in New York, and the individual, a physician himself, was in-
toxicated at the time he was bitten, and died in two hours.

We reached the Hondo, a tributary of the Mueces [Nueces],[7]
about noon, and unsaddled where there was a little knoll,
shaded by trees, in the middle of the ravine. There was no
running water, but a good supply was found not far off, and
we set about preparing dinner. Just then, we were interrupted
by the arrival of the scouting party of twenty who had been
hunting the Indians;[8] they have been gone over two days, and
were returning to take a better start. As they turned their
horses out, and spread themselves on the side of the river, I
thought I had never realized so fully how far I was removed
from the usages of conventional life—nowhere, in all my wide
wanderings had I seen a picture of such wild outlawdom—for
outlaws they really are, because the government fails to protect
them; and they had assembled with such arms as they could
hastily gather, leaving their cattle to stray and their cornfields
to waste, to obey the first law of Nature.

Strolling up the creek, I saw a large Mocasin [*sic*] snake
shelter itself under a heap of dry drift wood, and I set it on
fire. The snake perished by the fire, rather than attempt to
escape; but there ran out a blue rat, which I killed. It was a
species that was new to me, and indigenous to the country.
The gray rat, so common in all sea ports, and originally from

---

[7] The Hondo flows into the Frio, which joins the Nueces. Perhaps Stillman felt
that constituted being a tributary. More likely he was simply mistaken about the
Hondo being a tributary of the Nueces. *Ibid.*, I, pp. 650, 831.

[8] Because of constant Indian raids south and west of San Antonio during 1855,
several patrol forces, including one under Captain James H. Callahan, had been
organized. See Governor Elisha M. Pease to Callahan, July 5, 1855, in Dorman H.
Winfrey and James M. Day (eds.), *Indian Papers of Texas and the Southwest, 1825-
1916,* 5 vols. (Austin: Pemberton Press, 1966), III, pp. 220-21.

Europe, has not yet found its way so far as San Antonio, and this one avoids the habitation of man. From its throat I perceived a black larva of some insect, about to make its exit. It was about an inch long, and a half inch in diameter. It is known by the name of "wolf," and infests stock as well as small animals. It was a hideous looking creature, and I kept it to allow it to develope under my own eye. We resumed our journey about the middle of the afternoon, and travelled about twenty miles to the Rio Frio. The country over which we rode does not differ materially from that which we passed over in the morning, though the chapparel is more abundant on the hills. This chapparel is composed of a great variety of small-leaved thorny shrubs, with rigid branches, and is impenetrable to man or beast. They form in themselves a complete study for a botanist, and the rabbit, quail, and rattlesnake make them their favorite resort. In the wide-spread valleys the grass is long and mesquet brushes interrupt the sight; deer were to be seen scattered through them at frequent intervals, but never in large herds as on the plains near the coast. Arrived at the Frio, we saw an Indian lodge, some months deserted. This river is a fine, clear, running stream, with cypress trees growing along its margin, and with high wooded banks. We crossed, and camped on the elevated plain on the opposite side. We were agreeably surprised to find here a hunter, named Forester,[9] with a small party, and an ox team. We had followed his trail all day, and wondered who, besides ourselves could be travelling with wheels in this unfrequented region. The trees around his waggon were hung with carcasses of deer and wild turkeys. As we had not hunted, he sent us a fine turkey. Sandy and myself went to the river to catch fish, but though there was an abundance of fine fish there, the gars, those rapacious half fish

---

[9] Probably F. Forester, a German Immigrant who, with his wife Louisa, lived in Comal County. Carpenter, *Texas Federal Population Schedule,* II, p. 572.

and half aligators [*sic*] would destroy our hooks, and we caught nothing. It was dark when we unsaddled, and we ate a late supper by the light of our camp fire. In the morning, a young buck came close to camp, and stood still to be shot. The hams only were taken, and the remainder was left to the vulture. Forester shot here a large Jaguar, the fiercest and most beautiful of the feline race in America.

From the Frio to the Leona there was no recent trail. For seven miles we rode over a plain which had been recently burned off, and the half-burned trees were yet smoking except the narrow strips of land which skirted the river, and in which we had passed the night, the whole distance was a wide blackened waste, the dried trees were consumed and the living were blasted and drained by the Leona. For many miles we saw only trees, even as far as the eye could reach, and through these we could trace the windings of the river by the superior growth of the trees on its banks. As we descended, we soon became buried in a low growth of Mesquets. The soil was rich and low, grass thin, and weeds rank. It is called bottom land— just the place for those savage beasts after which it takes its name, Leona. For three miles before we reach the river, it is nearly flat, and the old road, which our Ranger had travelled during the border wars, was with difficulty distinguished, even by his practised eye, and had often to be abandoned from the thickets which had grown up in it, and the sloughs that traverse it. Before we reached the river I was in a worse condition than those who excited my sympathy so much in the scouting party we met on the Hondo. While dodging one limb, another would bear away a trophy from my back. We chose our camping ground in a bend of the river, nearly cut off from the main land by a lagoon. The banks of the river are low, and covered with live oaks and ash trees, with the thorny vines of the *smilax* interwoven with the undergrowth that makes it difficult of access, and we chose the best position for shade that we could find. Two miles above us, on the other side of the river, lived a man named Westfall.[10] For four years he has dwelt alone, thirty miles from any settler, and out of the way of any travel-ler. He is well known in Western Texas as Leather-stocking; we were anxious to reach his house, and leave there the carriage, which we could carry no farther; but the old bridge had been carried away, and there was a necessity to construct another. It was too late to attempt anything that day, and we hunted and fished with indifferent success. Tracks of the bear and other wild animals were plenty in the mud of the river bank, and we scattered ourselves about for the night, feeling secure from Indians in a region so long deserted by both red and white men, and trusting to a fire to protect us from any other foes.

Musquitoes [*sic*], so numerous on the coast, are rare at this distance from it, but parasitic insects infest the thickets on the banks of the river. A kind that I have never been able to detect with the naked eye, bury themselves under the skin, and cause an irritation that continues for weeks, unless they are killed by the application of oil or other remedy. Wood ticks are very plenty, and I occupied myself until I fell asleep in picking them from me, and throwing them over to the judge, who had some hundred pounds of flesh to spare.

J.D.B.S.

---

10 Edward Dixon Westfall was a friend of William A. A. (Big Foot) Wallace and a renowned Indian fighter who was born in Knox County, Indiana, on December 22, 1820. He moved to Texas in 1845 and, after service in the Mexican War, established himself on the banks of the Leona River more than 100 miles southwest of San Antonio. A. J. Sowell, *Early Settlers and Indian Fighters of Southwest Texas* (Austin: Ben C. Jones & Co., Printers, 1900), pp. 353; see also Webb, Carroll and Branda (eds.), *Handbook of Texas,* I, p. 188.

The Crayon (New York), II (September 26, 1855), pp. 193-95.

Wanderings in the Southwest
No. VII

The morning dawned with an east wind, and a slight fall of rain upon our faces awoke us. The Judge, Sandy, and Sechio, rode back on our trail some miles, to visit some land located in the vicinity to which the judge held a claim. It was expected that I should have a good supply of fish for dinner against their return. In the clear, blue waters of the river, I could see fine fish, but they would not take the hook.

I remembered that the day before I had followed the report of a couple of guns to a lagoon, some distance from the camp, and found Sandy and Sechio had fired upon a snake bird (*Plotus*), and were watching on the bank to see the dead bird rise to the surface, while the curious animal was watching them with its head just out of water at a safe distance. Knowing that the bird is a fish feeder, I did not doubt that I could catch fish where he could. I found the place, and threw in my line, just where the darter fell; nor did I wait long; my little blue and red float disappeared from the surface. I had no reel, and the struggles that followed were decided by physical strength, in which science had no part; nevertheless, I think it would have delighted your piscatorial friend the "Angler,"[1] to have had a hand in it. I secured one green perch, known here as trout, weighing about four pounds, and lost my hooks. Returning to camp, I got a very large hook and stronger line, and landed fish enough for three days' consumption. At length my large hook gave out under the weight of a huge cat fish. More earnest fishing one will not often see. There were indica-

---

1 "Angler" was probably another correspondent for *The Crayon.*

tions of rain, and I returned with my game just in time to wake up the camp guard, and protect our stores from a heavy fall of rain.

About three o'clock, the party who had been out returned, having been bewildered in the chapparel, denuded by thorns, and but for the instincts of Sechio, would not have been able to find the camp. They reported that the trail of a dozen horses had followed ours down to the bottom, when it was lost. Had the party been white men, they would have come into camp, as our waggon trail told who we were, and their avoiding us, after following it so far as to ascertain just where we were, made it certain that they were foes. It was determined to lose no time in effecting a crossing of the river. The stream is about one-third the size of the San Antonio, at the town of that name, but its channel is miry and destitute of a ford. The old bridge had been carried away, and it was necessary to construct one sufficiently strong to carry our horses over. An axe soon cleared away the young trees that had grown up in the way, and several, sufficiently long to serve as string-pieces, were prepared. A few hours more of daylight would have enabled us to cross to the high grounds of the west bank; but night set in with lowering clouds threatening rain. A good supply of dry wood was gathered preparatory to a wet night. A line was drawn between two trees, to which one edge of a pair of blankets was pinned, while the other was staked to the ground, to windward, to protect our heads, and a huge fire blazed at our feet. The horses were picketed in a semi-circle outside of the camp. I volunteered to stand the first watch, and when the last man had taken his place on the ground, I took my seat on a fallen tree, about one hundred yards beyond the horses, having them between me and the lights of our fire. The night was very dark, as dark as a rainy, moonless night might be, and the red glare of the fire on the surrounding trees, with the sparks reeling through the branches, made the darkness beyond and around more fearful. I thought to a certainty that the savages would make an attempt to steal our horses on the first opportunity, and my hand was constantly on my six shooter, and my eye was alternately peering into the blackness on one side, and surveying the dark outline that intervened between me and the fire on the other. The wind and rain increased, and about midnight it began to fall in torrents, without thunder or lightning. The cry of nocturnal beast and bird was hushed in the steady roar of the falling rain. I went to the fire to pile on a fresh supply of fuel. My companions slept soundly, and I resumed my station for another hour, when I called Sechio to relieve me, and lay down with my head on the meal-bag under the blanket, and was soon asleep. When I awoke I found myself enveloped in the blanket, which the wind had blown down, the water had extinguished the fire, and it was so dark that I could not tell the direction of the place where it had been. I called to Sechio, but he had abandoned his post, and taken refuge in the wagon. The torrents fell even more determined[ly] than before. Blankets offered no protection, but only weighed me down.

It had occurred to me when we came to this river, that the proper channel could hold but a small part of the water that must flow through it at certain times, and it seemed to me impossible that it could carry off even that which fell in our immediate vicinity now, and if this rain was as general as the length of time it had been falling, would lead us to think a flood was inevitable, but the utter helplessness of our position in such darkness kept me still, until Sandy spoke. "Is not this an awful rain," said he. "Yes," said I, "and I have been thinking what we shall do if the river overflows." "There is no danger; I have been camped just above this, when it rained for eight days, and it did not overflow." We thought no more

of Indians; no sane Indian would come into this bottom on
such a night, and for myself I could not banish the conviction
that there was great danger of being drowned before daylight.
We know that the love of life is not equally strong in all individuals, but I do not remember ever to have seen a man who
had not a choice as to the mode of his death. The thought of
being drowned like a kitten, and floated away into an unknown
wilderness, forced itself upon me with an appalling reality. I
listened to the rushing of the water, and fancied myself striking out for some invisible land, grasping at shrubs and shadows
as I was swept by, and longing for one gleam of daylight to
reveal the true state of things about us.

This was bad enough, the low places were full of water, and
the rubbish was drifting past us in a direction parallel to the
river. We saw the brands of our last night's fire floating about
us, our guns under water. Air bubbled up from the ground
with a noise of rushing water. The horses were snorting with
impatience and terror, floundering in the mud and water, and
seemed to have a better conception of the danger which surrounded them than their masters. The Judge still slept, though
the water was lifting each corner of his mattress. Sechio slept
in the wagon, Antonio leaned drowsily against a tree, having
not been fully awake. The time had come for some decided
action. "We must get to higher ground," said I to Sandy, "or
we shall all drown."

"There is no higher ground within three miles, and we shall
have to cross several sloughs now full of water, and the horses
will mire everywhere," he replied. The conclusion was, that
when driven to it we must get into trees. The Judge was now
fully roused, and having satisfied himself that the river had
overflown its banks, determined to make an attempt to reach
higher ground. Word was given at once to saddle. Such things
as had not yet floated away were placed in the wagon, and

the latter was made fast to a tree, and we struck out each one
as he got ready, Sechio leading the way; the water was now
over the whole ground, and by floundering and swimming we
reached the margin of the first slough. Here the flood had
taken a short cut across the isthmus of the peninsula bend
where we had camped, and I paused to see how Sechio managed to reach the opposite bank. Shouts of distress were heard
in the rear, when presently Antonio's mule came swimming
past without his rider. I endeavored to arrest him but he seemed to think it every mule's, as well as every man's, duty to look
out for himself in emergencies like the present. One after the
other we all reached the side where Sechio stood, and followed
the road until we found land above water, when the horses
were turned loose, and we sat down on our saddles uncertain
how long we could be permitted to rest here. The rain still
poured down with unabated violence. We had neither food nor
the means of getting fire; and each one sat under his blanket
trembling with the long continued shower-bath that penetrated
to our skin. Sechio, after rescuing his friend Antonio, went out
in search of the trunk of a dead yucca, which contains a tinder
dry at all times, and with the flint lock rifle he struck a fire,
being protected by a blanket held over him, and with great
skill managed to get a fire started from the wet materials. Under
its influence our apathy gave way, and we all set to work to
collect fuel, which being piled up in a cone, one end of each
stick resting on the ground, served to shed off the water. Thus
we had an illustration of the superior resources of the untutor-
ed child of the woods to the science of the white man. The
rain moderated about noon, and at four o'clock the sun showed
us its face. But the water had surrounded us, and was within
a few inches of our camp. Everywhere out of the old road the
horses would sink down in the quicksand, and as well as ourselves were suffering for food. At night we cut bushes, and

piled them around the fire to sleep upon. The next morning the sun came out warm, and the forenoon was spent in drying and cleaning such arms as we had brought away with us in our hasty flight. I had saved only my revolver, secured by a belt to my waist, and I am certain that I should not have saved it had I not forgotten that it hung there, so I took Sechio's flint lock rifle to find some animal in the same unfortunate situation as ourselves, to relieve the cravings of hunger. Sandy went out in another direction with the same object. At the distance of a few rods I found a fresh track of deer, and followed it for some time in its crooked trail, until it occurred to me that if I should lose my way in such an homogeneous thicket, where I had no elevated landmarks in sight, it would be a serious accident. I took out my pocket compass, and found a variation of at least 180°! I appealed to the sun, but had no conception as to the time of day, and could not tell whether it was in the right place or not. I listened for some noise from camp, for I could not have gone beyond hearing, I shouted— there was no response. In despair I pulled out my "life preserver," and tried to fire one after the other all the barrels, but the dull click of the hammer told me that the capsules were all spoiled. I had no alternative but to follow my own tracks back. This was not difficult, for the most part, as the ground was soft; at length I came to a place where my steps were double, and I soon made so many that I could not distinguish the primitive ones, and I was in despair, when I saw the smoke of our fire, and the Judge asleep under the shade of a blanket. Having corrected the compass, I took a fresh start, and succeeded in finding a multitude more of deer tracks beside those of turkeys, a black bear, and a large feline, probably the panther, and at length after great exhaustion, during which the compass was constantly trying to deceive me, I succeeded in returning safely to camp. Sandy arrived soon after with a large doe, and our apprehensions of starvation gave way as steak after steak was broiled on the coals and disposed of without salt. What remained was cut into continuous strips, and hung over the fire to dry for future use. We all felt well enough now to laugh, and Texas once more appeared as a "glorious country." It appears incomformable with the law of progress, that man should never be satisfied with his condition, and we had no sooner had a sufficiency of vension than we desired some salt on the next we ate. The next morning the river was reported fallen, and Antonio was to make the attempt to reach the wagon, and if possible bring off some small stores that were regarded as indispensable. He was a good swimmer, and he took the best horse. A bag containing bacon, another with cornmeal, another with coffee, and sugar, and salt, were to be brought out if possible. Sandy urged him not to forget the coffee and his box of cigars, the Judge wanted some tobacco that was in his carpet bag hanging on a tree. I had no request to make, my saddlebags containing my instruments, collections, my sketch book, wallet, in fact all the valuables I had with me, I had seen placed on the seat of the waggon above everything else, and the worst that could happen to it was to get wet, and I had rather trust it there than with him. He had been gone for several hours, when we heard him shouting and the horse snorting, as though nearly exhausted. The bushes prevented us from seeing what was passing, but Sechio ran to the aid of his friend, while Sandy followed the sound of the horse, which had reached one side of the flood, but was floundering among the thickets and bogs below the road. He was brought in with a remnant of the meal bag hanging to the pommel of his saddle. For a long time we heard the Mexicans struggling in the water, and at length Antonio came with the loss of his shirt, and empty handed. "Where," said Sandy with consternation, "is the coffee?" "With your cigars," replied Antonio, pointing down the river. "Cigars!" said the Judge, "why did you overload him with your cigars!" The loss of the coffee was a harder blow than the loss of a horse would have been. It is almost the only luxury the woodsman knows. Soon after Sechio came up from an ineffectual attempt to recover the Judge's carpet bag. "Have you lost my carpet bag with my clothes, razors, maps, and everything?" and his mind seemed to be lost in taking an inventory of all the little articles of comfort it contained. "And you loaded him with your carpet bag too?" said Sandy, as he pulled off one of his shoes to give to Antonio. I laughed at the retort, although the next announcement was, that all the articles on the waggon seat were carried away by the upsetting of the same. The water subsided so rapidly that the next morning we visited the ground of our unlucky camp, and searched for the missing articles, but found nothing of value that could float. I picked up a living specimen of an *achatina,* that is new to me and rare here. The shell is about two inches long and pale white. I have occasionally met with the dead shell, but this was the first living one, and it is the only specimen of any kind that I have from our excursion.

We extricated our wagon, and had no alternative but to return with all despatch [*sic*]. We were glad to get on higher ground, and breathe purer air. The plains that were burned off, and were so sterile when we crossed them, were now green with the young shoots of grass. The quail was just revisiting the haunts where she had left her young brood to the flames, and the wild turkey ran like a thief with nothing to hide him from our eye. Wild horses had returned, and scoured the plain with mane and tail streaming in the wind, and deer stood still quietly watching us, grey as the shadows of twilight that were gathering when we again reached our old camp on the Frio. I was surprised to find this river had not risen, but Sandy said the time for it had not come, and determined upon ford-

ing it that night, late as it was. I am informed that it rose soon
after, and was not fordable for some days. We camped in a fine
grassy valley, about a mile from the river, and Sechio came in
soon after with a turkey. "Why," asked Sandy, "have you shot
a setting turkey?" The boy replied, "what for she run?" It
was a good change, poor as it was and saltless, from the dried
deer meat. Two days brought us again to the rancho on the
Medina, from which we started. Some time after our return,
we learned that three days after we left the Leona, a party of
twelve Lipans attacked the house of Westfall, or "Leather-
stocking," two miles from our camp, and shot him through
the lungs, and killed a guest. Westfall, after lying three days,
dragged himself to Fort Inge,[2] at the head of the river, thirty
miles distant.[3] There can be but little doubt that this was the
same party that followed our trail, and the date of this attack
corresponded with the time that it would have been possible
to have crossed the river.

J.D.B.S.

---

[2] Fort Inge was established on the east bank of the Leona River in 1849. In 1855
it consisted of perhaps a dozen buildings of various sizes and constructions. It was
named for Lieutenant Zebulon M. P. Inge, of the Second Dragoons, who was killed
at the battle of Resaca de la Palma. Webb, Carroll, and Branda (eds.), *Handbook of
Texas,* I, p. 627; Olmsted, *Journey Through Texas,* p. 285; and M. L. Crimmins (ed.)
"W. G. Freeman's Report on the Eighth Military Department," in *Southwestern Hist.
Quar.,* LIII (July 1949), pp. 74-77.

[3] After numerous Indian fights, Westfall was ambushed at his house on June 30,
1855. He was badly wounded, and his friend, a Frenchman named Louie, was killed.
After spending two nights in the cabin, Westfall summoned all his strength and made
his way to Fort Inge. He met a hunting party on the road, and they took him to
the Fort, where he received treatment for his wound. *San Antonio Herald,* July 10,
1855, p. 3, col. 1. Westfall died on June 12, 1897. Sowell, *Early Settlers,* pp. 363-67.

The Crayon (New York), III (January 1856), pp. 6-9.

Wanderings in the Southwest
Second Series, No. 1

An easterly wind in Western Texas portends rain, and such a wind was bearing along watery masses of cumuli in the direction which my road lay far beyond the limits of the last herdsman's cottage. At the inn kept by M. Tardé, at Castroville, I could look with resignation upon the storm that overtook me at that place. Here one sees for the last time the comforts of a home; he bids adieu to comfortable beds and the luxuries of the table until he finds himself, after many weary weeks, among the old settlements of New Mexico. A night of thunder and lightning and rain, was succeeded by a day of dull grey clouds, distilling a fine mist upon the ground already saturated. When I visited Castroville, four months before, the district court was in session, and the attachés gave it a busy air; now, the population were as quiet as a village in their native France. The martins, which had possession of the piazza, where they had reared their young and kept up an incessant chattering all day, had gone too, but the drouth that prevailed then had been succeeded by copious rains. Bean vines, under the training of the accomplished madam, had twined with extraordinary grace up the strings that covered the gable end and loaded down the barrel-stave white-washed fence,

". . . and the sweet tuberose,
The sweetest flower for scent that blows,"

hung in heavy masses around the ruined nest of the martins. Walks could be extended only into the garden, where a double row of the multicaulis mulberry made a very pretty avenue, which our enthusiastic host had already appropriated to a future banquet hall. We had another rainy night, and another grey

morning gave us no hope of a speedy improvement in the
weather, and it was deemed advisable to proceed. Fortunately,
for me I met here Capt. Ricketts,[1] of the 1st Artillery, on his
way to Fort Duncan.[2] As our road was the same for ninety
miles, I accepted a seat in his ambulance, and surrendered my
horse to a dragoon of his escort. We found our trains ready to
start, and standing in the mud, while the teamsters, with their
military great coats dripping with water, appeared reluctant to
start. The rains had been so violent that the contents of the
wagons were all wet, the covers having proved insufficient to
protect them, and the men, who for two nights had slept in
or under the wagons, seemed thoroughly watersoaked, and the
wagon-master of my train was so completely soaked with something stronger, that he was lying on the ground in a state of
insensibility. The captain ordered him to be taken out of the
mud and placed on one of his wagons.

Rainy days are rarely enjoyed by any travellers, but least of
all by those who are journeying over an unimproved country,
where the obstacles which nature everywhere opposes have
never been overcome by art; where it is often impossible to
stop, and to proceed is but little less difficult. Our ambulance
proceeded very well for a few miles over the hilly post-oak
country, but when it reached the rich flats on the Hondo, the
black loam and tangled grass loaded down the wheels, and a
distance of eight miles required as many hours to traverse it.
The heavier teams were left behind altogether. On the Hondo,

---

[1] Captain James B. Ricketts entered the army in 1839 as a Second Lieutenant.
After serving on the frontier, he fought with distinction at Bull Run, Cold Harbor,
and various other battles under General U. S. Grant in the Civil War. He retired in
1867 with the rank of Major General. Thomas H. S. Hamersly (comp.), *Complete
Regular Army Register of the United States: For One Hundred Years, (1779 to 1879)*
(Washington: T. H. S. Hamersly, 1880), p. 720.

[2] Fort Duncan, established on the left bank of the Rio Grande in 1849, was important in fighting the Indians on the frontier, and in the Mexican trade. Webb, Carroll,
and Branda (eds.), *Handbook of Texas,* I, pp. 624-25.

a man named Franks[3] has settled with a large number of negroes, and he had just opened, at his own expense, the road over which we travelled, connecting his crossing with Castroville. Mrs. F. was suffering intensely from a felon, and making use of a lancet which she furnished, I had the satisfaction of affording her relief. The place, a low, thatched cottage, with a stone house in process of building, was infested with dogs and negroes, and it was difficult to imagine where they all slept. A half dozen of the latter stood around while the captain and myself made the supplies of corn cakes and vension to disappear in such quick succession as to compel them to display their ivory. The cakes were made from corn just ripened, and grated on the cob, and I remember the relish with which I ate them, now that I have been for two months in the wilderness, with heartfelt emotion. Milk and butter, too—alas! We succeeded in reaching the Seco[4] about eleven o'clock at night. The train was all left behind and fast in the mud, and we were without our camp equipage, but we found a lodgment in the house of a German named Rider.[5] The rain had ceased, and the following day we made a short journey to the Sabinal,[6] in order to give time to the train to overtake us. It was a picturesque spot which was selected, and the wagons as they came up formed in a semicircle around the brow of a smooth hill, at the foot of which was the rocky bed of the stream, enlarged here into a deep and wide pond, where two or three large cypresses stood with their feet in the water, the last that we see going west; to

---

[3] Perhaps Christian Frank, age 30 in 1850, a German immigrant. Carpenter (ed.), *Texas Federal Population Schedule,* I, p. 183.

[4] Seco Creek was near Castroville. A small German settlement, Quihi, was located on Quihi Creek, a branch of the Seco. Olmsted, *Journey Through Texas,* p. 278.

[5] Perhaps John Rider, who was a 25 year old soldier stationed at Fort Martin Scott in 1850. Carpenter (ed.), *Texas Federal Population Schedule,* II, p. 838.

[6] The Sabinal River rises in southwestern Bandera County and flows into the Frio, some 58 miles southeastward. Webb, Carroll, and Branda (eds.), *Handbook of Texas,* II, p. 523.

the right of us was a grove of oaks, where the tents of some settlers were pitched. My train had not arrived, and I was dependent upon the hospitality of my generous friend. The county, as far as Fort Inge, presents but little of special interest; sometimes post-oak and at others mesquet trees predominated, but everywhere rich grass. The rivers are all mere brooks, without auxiliaries, making a deal of noise over the stones in channels much too large for them, or only furnishing water holes. The higher lands intervening begin to show chapparal [sic] and gravel, and the trees gradually appear smaller. The whirr of the quail is frequent, but the grouse is not seen west of San Antonio. At the head of the Leona Captain Ricketts left me, as from this point our routes diverge. Here I waited two days for my train. The head of the Leona, at the distance of thirty miles below which I had met with so disastrous a deluge, is in a wide flat of rich land, overgrown with thickets of small live oak, hackberry, and pecan trees. There can be no doubt that it will prove sickly when it becomes settled. I am much induced to believe the tradition that it is a new river. Its jungles are the haunts of innumerable deer and wild turkeys, and the puma, jaguar, and tiger cat roam unmolested. Mr. Black[7] has built a substantial stone building at the head of the river, and has laid out a town, which he calls Encina.[8] A forest of small elms (*Ulmus alata*) and live oaks throws a shadow over the site of the town, grateful in a country where, except on the rivers, one will hardly find trees with foliage heavy enough to afford a shade. Situated as it is on the great thoroughfare to Mexico, and the last suitable situation on good water, it will become an important place. I was agreeably surprised to see Captain

---

[7] Probably Reading Wood Black, who operated a lime kiln and two rock quarries near the head of the Leona River. *Ibid.*, I, p. 167.

[8] Encina was a small town in what is today Uvalde County. See entry for Reading Wood Black in *ibid*.

Walker[9] and his Lieut., Devant,[10] [*sic*] of the Mounted Rifles, ride up the same afternoon that my train arrived. They were returning to Fort Duncan, after a scout with twenty men, and their command was encamped at the deserted Fort two miles below. We made them a visit at their camp. Close to the Fort is a remarkable hill of volcanic rock, rising from the plain to the height of two hundred feet, in a conical form, and broken into irregular masses of rock. From the summit, several other similar hills are visible. These are the more remarkable because they are the only traces of irregular volcanic action that I have seen in Texas. The hospitality of a soldier's board is always free, and now, when I remember the right good will with which the table was loaded down, my gratitude is mingled with a deeper and sadder emotion in knowing that that accomplished gentleman and officer, Devant, found soon after a watery grave while crossing the Rio Grande. I returned to Black's about ten o'clock at night, and found my wagon-master lying in the road drunk, and covered with blood, from the effects of a fight in which he had indulged with one of his men, and as on the following morning he was unable to proceed, I left him. Just before starting, a party of fillibusters [*sic*] came in from Eagle Pass with a negro that they had captured in Mexico.[11] This man was a fine-looking mulatto, who had been twice captured before; on one occasion, his captor arrested him on the Texas

---

9 Captain John G. Walker entered the Mounted Rifles with the rank of First Lieutenant in 1847 and was soon decorated for valiant conduct at San Juan de los Llanos during the Mexican War. Hamersly, *Register,* p. 835.

10 Brevet Second Lieutenant William M. Davant, of South Carolina, entered the Mounted Rifles July 1, 1854, and served until he drowned October 1, 1855. Francis B. Heitman (comp.), *Historical Register and Dictionary of the United States Army* (Washington: Govt. Printing Office, 1903), I, p. 355. See also *Official Army Register for 1855* (Washington: Adj. Gen. Office, 1855), p. 14.

11 The filibusters that Stillman encountered probably were led by W. R. Henry, who had announced his intention of going to Mexico to foment a revolution. The *San Antonio Texan,* Aug. 9, 1855, p. 2, col. 4, reported that he had left for the border. The *Texas State Gazette* (Austin), Aug. 11, 1855, p. 2, col. 4, printed his remarks, made

side, while the negro was waiting for the means to cross the river, and on his way to San Antonio he sold his claim on him for $50, but the negro, watching his opportunity, escaped with his captor's horse and six-shooter. He was followed across the Rio Grande and again seized, and badly burned in the struggle that ensued, but his cries called in the natives and his persecutor was compelled to effect his own escape. Once afterwards he was captured, and his captor had him at work at Encina, waiting an opportunity to send him to his master, when he escaped, and a suit was then pending, his master vs. his captor, for his services, as a punishment for permitting him to escape, when his third capture by the fillibusters put an end to it. He was safe now, with a pistol always ready to shoot him down at the slightest pretext. Poor fellow! he deserved a better fate. These fillibusters, in their efforts to extend the area of freedom, were refused admission by the insurgent Mexicans, who declared them a nuisance, but they succeeded so far as to re-capture this heroic slave. Nine miles brought us to the Nueces, at that time a clear, rapid stream, and difficult to ford. Here was encamped the advance party of Major Emory's boundary commission,[12] camped at the head springs of Turkey Creek.[13] There is good land and picturesque scenery along this creek, but away from it the land is rolling, stony, and covered

---

preparatory to crossing the Rio Grande. The *San Antonio Herald,* Aug. 14, 1855, p. 2, col. 1, reported that he and forty or fifty others had been arrested by the Mexican authorities. Henry and his band had returned to San Antonio by the end of August (*San Antonio Texan,* Aug. 30, 1855, p. 2, col. 3), and *The Texas State Times* (Austin), Sept. 1, 1855, p. 2, col. 1, observed that the Mexicans did not want his help. Olmsted also encountered such a party during his trip to Mexico. See Olmsted, *Journey Through Texas,* pp. 256-57; Ronnie C. Tyler, "The Callahan Expedition of 1855: Indians or Negroes?" *Southwestern Hist. Quar.,* LXX (April 1967), pp. 574-85; Ronnie C. Tyler, "Fugitive Slaves in Mexico," *Journal of Negro History,* LVII (January 1972), pp. 1-12.

12 The Boundary Survey Commission was in the process of marking the boundary between the United States and Mexico following the war of 1846. William H. Emory was the commissioner, replacing John Russell Bartlett. See Goetzmann, *Army Exploration,* p. 183.

with shrubs. Another day's ride over a country sterile and every hour more desolate, brought me to Fort Clark,[14] at the head of a beautiful stream called Las Morus [*sic*].[15] The river rises a few rods above the Fort, and bursts out, Minerva-like, at once in its full proportions, and is overshadowed by very large pecans and oaks, which define the outline of its course through a region which is else where almost destitute of trees. Dr. Norris,[16] the accomplished surgeon at this post, told me that he had known the stream to rise a foot in a single day, with no apparent cause; a proof of the great distance at which it has its subterranean source. It affords another example of this interesting feature of many of the streams of Western Texas. From this point of the road one bids a long adieu to forest shades and quiet waters. We have the beautiful behind us. On my arrival an express was sent to a detachment of dragoons, which came down as an escort to Major Emory's party, on their return to El Paso,[17] to wait for further orders. I made my adieus to the officers over a watermelon, and in an ambulance, with four grey mules, provided by the efficient quartermaster, I drove out to the Pedras [Piedras?] Pintos, a small brook eight miles distant, where the escort were camped.

---

13 Among the at least twenty-three Turkey Creeks in Texas, one rises in what is today southern Dawson County and flows into the Nueces River. *Johnson's New Map;* Webb, Carroll, and Branda (eds.), *Handbook of Texas,* II, p. 808.

14 Established in 1852, Fort Clark was located at the head of Las Moras Creek in Kinney County. Webb, Carroll, and Branda (eds.), *Handbook of Texas,* I, p. 622.

15 Los Morus (Moras?) is an intermittent stream that rises in central Kinney County and flows thirty miles southward into the Rio Grande in northwestern Maverick County. *Ibid.,* II, p. 34; *Johnson's New Map.*

16 Dr. Basil Norris (surgeon at Fort Clark) entered the army in 1852 with the rank of First Lieutenant. He was decorated after the battle of Vicksburg and was promoted to Brevet Colonel in 1865. Hamersly, *Register,* p. 666.

17 El Paso (present-day Ciudad Juárez) was the Mexican village on the right bank of the Rio Grande. The Treaty of 1848 with Mexico declared that the boundary line would be drawn north of El Paso. Later, the Mexican city changed its name to Ciudad Juárez, and the American village of Franklin assumed the name of El Paso. Webb, Carroll, and Branda (eds.), *Handbook of Texas,* I, pp. 561-62.

Ten dragoons, armed with rifles, and variously dressed, with red shirts and blue, one wears a black wool hat without a crown, another a light one with half a rim, a third with a hat entire, tied with a deerskin in band, turned up before and behind, and drawn over the ears. The sergeant has a straw hat, with a band of broadcloth fancifully cut full of holes, and notched on the margins. He wears fustian breeches, and has killed a deer and sat in the blood. They all have good horses, and the brass mountings of their saddles, the glitter of their rifles, carried uniformly, no less than their orderly march, betray the disciplined soldier, despite their ununiform dress. They are followed by two wagons, carrying their forage, each drawn by six mules. A third wagon, like the two preceeding, is loaded with forage for my mules and its own. It rumbles along just in front of me, with a long, narrow bucket swinging to the hind axle; a chain to lock the wheels in steep descents, dangles along the road; then the ambulance, with a driver with long hair, broad-brimmed hat, and broader shoulders, and a detachment of one man of the 1st Infantry, as my body guard, sits with him. Two more dragoons, as rear-guard, complete the train. It was the last day of summer that we set out. The cool nights had deposited myriads of crystal globules on the points of the long, coarse grass that covered the low ground where the creek found its course, now overgrown by it, and now widening into a little pond, where a few cat-tail flags outranked the grass on its margin. Blackbirds chattered among them, red-winged and yellow-headed—this last variety are very common in Texas. Slowly we wend our way over smooth rock roads, the mules wag their long ears as they walk, the tar-bucket swings, and the chain dangles on over the weary road. Though the ascent has been gradual, the elevation must be considerable, judging from the aspect of the country. The rolling surface is scantily covered with soil, hardly sufficient to cover the solid limestone below it, but isolated bushes are spread over it, some in lively green, others with a whitish foliage, and crowded with tubular flowers of a bright rose color. The yucca grows small, but is too characteristic a plant to escape notice, interspersed as it is everywhere among the mottled shrubbery. In the lower country, it has a trunk resembling the palm tree, but wherever found on the table lands, its leaves start from the root, are from a yard to a yard and a half long, concave above, convex below, with sharp smooth edges, terminating in a hardened point; they are so rigid as to resist a blow from a club, and standing out in every direction, like radii, from a centre, they would form a *chevaux-de-frise* so complete as to impale any animal that would attempt to force it. As a fence, they would be impassable; and so formidable do they look, that two of them planted at a gate would be equivalent, in my estimation, to a watchdog. We camped the second night on the San Filippe,[18] a clear but cheerless stream. My tent is pitched facing the fire, by a detachment of the dragoons assisted by the infantry. A cot, a trunk, and a camp table are placed in it. I had obtained from the commissary such stores as were necessary for the road, coffee, sugar, bacon, and hard bread, which last furnished me an excellent field for entomological researches. If I have anything better I must depend upon somebody's gun. There are Texas quail (*Ortyx texana*)[19] in plenty, and fish seemed to be abundant in a deep place in the creek, where it expanded into a pond, at the base of a limestone cliff. A musket served me for a shot gun, and I had hooks and lines. I baited the hook with a small mullet, and left it for the larger ones to take at

---

18 San Felippe (Felipe) Creek rises in southeastern Val Verde County and flows eleven miles into the Rio Grande near Del Rio. *Ibid.*, II, p. 550.

19 Illustrated in Spencer F. Baird, "Birds of the Boundary," in William H. Emory, *Report on the United States and Mexican Boundary Survey* 34th Cong., 1st Sess., S. E. D. 108, 2 vols. (Washington: A. O. P. Nicholson, Printer, 1847, 1859), II, Pt. 2. plate xxiv.

their leisure, to try the more exciting sport of the field. The sudden flush of a flock of quails startles me, and before I can recover my presence of mind they are beyond range, but I see where they settle, and creep carefully up to the spot; they are just crowding to the border of a pile of prickly pears, and ready to fly. The trigger yielded to the pressure of the finger, and I thought the gun would refuse to perform its office, but at length it did "go," and so did an indefinite number of birds. I ran to the spot, expecting to find half their number dead upon the field; the cactus was bleeding at every pore, but my hopes of dinner had flown, leaving me no feather as a souvenir. I found them again, but the cap would not explode, and as night came on I returned to the stream where I had left my line, but the bait was gone and left nothing better in its place. Returned to camp and dined on bacon and pilot bread, as usual.

The next morning I returned to the attack on the quails, and succeeded in wounding one, but when I went to pick it up, it rose and flew so high that it seemed as though it was resolved never to have any more to do with this treacherous world. Returned to camp and breakfasted on biscuit and bacon.

This day unfolded still more clearly the interesting geological features of the country. The undulations of the surface deepened into ravines, showing the stratifications of limestone; the hills are almost denuded of soil, the bushes still more stunted. Away to the left is the fantastic outline of mountains in Mexico, rising in acute angles and perpendicular walls to the clouds, but all distant and dimly blue.

Suddenly a cañon yawns below us, and the train with locked wheels descends between two walls of rock, some of the strata of which are of great thickness, and undermined by the disintegration of the softer strata, and often worn by water from above into buttresses, and resembling some grim fortress towering hundreds of feet high. No trees, and only here and there a shrub in the lowest parts of the ravines, but everywhere bare blue rocks, vast, dreary, and desolate. Our wagons pitched and bounded over the loose rocks in the bottom of the cañon, until it spread into a larger one with a smooth stone floor, over which flowed, in a thin, broad sheet, the waters of "Devil's river."[20] I had approached a stream with such an ominous name with feelings of curiosity, but now I felt more of awe. Whether that name had been given it from the character of the savages who found in its inaccessible cliffs and caves a safe refuge from pursuit, and safe positions from which to shoot, their feathered, noiseless messengers of death upon a weaker party, or whether it was really a damned river, and consigned to the Prince of Darkness, I had formed no opinion. But I kept a sharp look out for all sorts of evil ones. The rock over which the water flowed was white from sulphur, apparently, and once my heart came into my throat at the sight of a hideous spotted saurian, with horns over its eyes, and a sharp tail, but it proved to be only the horned frog, and the normal condition of things was resumed under my jacket, without serious consequences.[21] Leaving the bed of the river, we crossed a ridge of hills to the ravine of another stream emptying into Devil's river, and camped on the open ground beyond. This camp ground is well known as that of the "Painted Caves."[22] Caves are everywhere common in the limestone cliffs, and most common in the highest and most inaccessible places. The mode of their formation appears to me very easy of solution.

---

[20] Devil's River, or Rio San Pedro, rises in northeastern Crockett County and flows southward for about 100 miles through Schleicher, Sutton, and Val Verde counties to pour into the Rio Grande. *Ibid.,* I, p. 495.

[21] Illustrated in Spencer F. Baird, "Reptiles of the Boundary," in Emory, *United States and Mexican Boundary Survey,* II, Pt. 2, plate 28.

[22] The Painted Caves that Stillman saw were thoroughly documented by Forrest Kirkland and his wife, Lula, in the 1930s. Reproductions of many of the images are printed in W. W. Newcomb, Jr., *The Rock Art of Texas Indians* (Austin: Univ. of Tex. Press, 1967), pp. 37-80.

They occur in that quality of limestone which I have compared before to the Caen stone. The effect of rain upon it is to harden it, but where it is exposed to the action of the atmosphere, and guarded from rain, it suffers disintegration. When a rock becomes detached and rolls down from its place, it may happen that a portion of the surface exposed is protected from the rain, and in process of time an excavation of considerable extent is found. There are great numbers of these caves in the cliffs, near where I am now writing, (on the Pecos[23]), of all sizes, from that of a baker's oven to that of a chamber where a hundred persons could find shelter. A shell of rock hangs down in front of them like a curtain, and the floor, which is always ascending, is covered with the debris as it falls in laminae and dust. Outside the rock is blue, from exposure to weather, but within it is a delicate yellow tint, the natural color of the stone. The painted caves are of this nature, but being easy of access and near an important crossing they had evidently been, from remote times, a resort of the savages who still hold dominion in these regions. My driver said "that when he first visited the place, five years since, the walls were covered with drawings in red and black, of men and animals," but every person visiting the spot seems to have conceived it his duty to leave some testimonial of his taste and intelligence in charcoal on the walls, until there are none of the natives' symbolical records remaining, except one or two too low to be conveniently reached. These caves were a mile from our camp, and not desiring to go further alone, I returned for a companion, and took a young Irishman, named Andy, a driver, to

---

[23] Rising in the Santa Fé, New Mexico, Mountain range, the Pecos River flows 260 miles southeastward to the Texas border. It passes through Loving and Reeves, Reeves and Ward, Ward and Pecos, Pecos and Crane, Pecos and Crockett, and Crockett and Ferrall counties, forming the boundary lines between them. It enters Val Verde County before flowing into the Rio Grande. Webb, Carroll, and Branda (eds.), *Handbook of Texas*, II, p. 355.

accompany me further down the river, where the scenery seemed
still more sublimely desolate. There was no running water, but
it stood in holes in the bed of the stream. We had gone about
half a mile below the caves when I discovered recent signs of
Indians, perhaps two or three days old, which I mentioned
to Andy. I proposed to him that if he should see a large mass
of coarse black hair anywhere behind the rocks, he should fire
upon it with his rifle, and I would reserve my buck-shot to
repulse a charge until he could re-load, but Andy remembered
that his mules required his attention, and wished to leave me
with both guns! But I insisted upon seeing him safely back to
camp. Andy, however, thought he saw his animals straying, I
fancy, and I soon lost sight of him behind a point of rocks.
Desolate as this region is, it is not wanting in the picturesque.
To an artist it could furnish studies of rock that it would be
difficult to excel.[24] Andy left me just at a very interesting spot—
a pond of deep, limpid water, into which projects a cliff of
solid stone, forty feet high, flat on the top, and undermined
by the force of the current when the water was high, in finely
curved lines, from top to bottom. Its connection with the prec-
ipices behind it was concealed by a few persimmon trees—the
only trees in sight. It seemed that I could catch some fish from
the top of this rock, but in the effort to gain it, I missed my
footing, and fell into a prickly pear, which gave me useful
employment till dark, in clearing my skin from the prickles.
Dined again on hard bread and bacon. Near the camp, at the
edge of the water, was a shrub common in all the streams of
this region, which resembles willow, and is generally called

---

[24] In the first half of the nineteenth century, science and art had much in common,
and artists considered it as much their responsibility as scientists to discover and
interpret the truths of nature. This concept led, for various reasons, to exact depiction
of many of the elements of nature, including rocks, which were key to the under-
standing of the geology of the earth. Stillman's comment should be viewed in this
context. See Barbara Novak, *Nature and Culture: American Landscape and Painting,
1825-1875* (N. Y: Oxford Univ. Press, 1980), pp. 47-77.

such, but it has composite flowers in a panicle. Upon one of
them a very large *Cicada* was making more noise than seemed
necessary, and I captured him. There is a smaller species of it
common in the North, and is often improperly called a locust,
by those who confound the true locust with the grasshopper. I
found, also, a fine specimen of the green Mantis, a very interesting insect, with a body about three inches long. Shot a
pigeon for my breakfast. In the effort to shoot a long-eared
rabbit, I was wounded by the point of the Yucca, and crippled
for two days. On the road the sergeant killed a fine buck. All
day we journeyed over the rolling table lands, now destitute
of every species of shrub; instead were clumps of the *Dasylyrion,*
a rigid, bearded, linear-leaved plant, which throws up from its
centre a spike from six to twelve feet high, which, in its season,
bore its flowers, but it was now dry; it is known as the bear
grass. As the road passes over the higher ground, the eye
ranges for many miles over a dreary, expanse of loose stones,
and the dry stalks of the "bear grass." Twenty-four miles brought
us to the first water. This is stagnant in a ravine. My attention
was called to a little spot by the road-side, full of mournful
interest, which awakened memories of that eventful year when
so many found uncoffined graves on that long journey to the
land of gold.[25] A small heap of stones told where a young girl
was left in a nameless grave. The teamster knows the spot and
the wolf howls her requeim. My tent could not be pitched
for the want of sufficient soil to receive the stakes, and I slept
in the ambulance, but there was a mule tied to each wheel, and
as it was a long time since I slept in a cradle, I found my situation about as comfortable as might be supposed. The following
day we ascended another long cañon, down, down until we
find ourselves again at the Devil's river, much nearer its source;
but the channel is still deep, and the banks, rising about as

[25] Stillman's trip to California.

high as the Highlands of the Hudson, are rounded and interrupted by ravines, but the stratification is nowhere concealed.
The bottom of the river is covered with rounded masses of
stone and thickets of small trees. We camped near where the
river widened into a small lake, on the margin of which a
grove of pecans had grown to a great size. Wild turkeys resort
to them at night. As the sun went down I planted myself near
them to take a turkey when he came in to roost, but the pecans
were lying thick around me, and I employed my time in picking them up until I gathered a peck, which so well satisfied me
that I returned to camp, but I paid dear for them. The *Rhus* or
poison-oak, covered the ground beneath the trees, but as I had
often exposed myself to it along the river bottoms of Texas and
California with impunity, I gave no attention to it, but it was
long before I could forget it. A turkey, a fawn, and some fish,
were taken by the men. The road from this crossing continues
up the bed of the river, which soon becomes lost in the rocks.
The mules labor hard among the round stones which are left
in heaps by the water after heavy rains. Camped at the head
of the valley near a pond called Beaver Lake.[26] A large flock of
turkeys flew away into a thicket of small live oaks. I saw
where one alighted in a dead tree, and with great difficulty
worked my way through the tall weeds that intervened, until
I reached the spot where I expected to see the turkey; a large
bird was perched at long range, and thinking it to be the bird I
was after, I fired, and away flew a fish-hawk with one leg
dangling below him, and at the same instant flew the turkey,
from a tree directly over my head, with both legs in good order.
I appeased my vexation by shooting three teal on the pond, and
determined to have my satisfaction by waylaying them when
they came in to roost. But in this I had as little success, though I

---

[26] Beaver Lake is a natural lake on Devil's River in extreme northern Val Verde
County. Webb, Carroll, and Branda (eds.), *Handbook of Texas,* I, p. 133.

spent two hours in a dense thicket where they ought to have come. Others were more successful, however, and more turkeys were slain than we could use. The succeeding day we again reached the table lands, if those can be called lands which are little else than rock. There we saw the first prairie-dog-town. This was to me an object of great interest, one which had been associated in my mind with the adventures of Clark and Lewis,[27] and the far interior of the great West, destined to be, for ages to come, as it had been from time immemorial, the home of the savage.

These are landmarks that are necessary to make one realize how far he has wandered from the land where sleep our fore-fathers who heard the war-cry of the Indian. But, independently of associations, the prairie-dog is an interesting animal. This community was small and limited by the nature of the ground. A small valley or depression in the ground had received the alluvium from the higher ground about it, to the depth, appar-ently, of several feet, and into which the marmot can readily excavate his burrow. They dig them a rod or more distant from each other, and never appear to stray far away, for, except in these, they have no protection from birds of prey, as well as wolves. They feed on the short, fine grass that seems to be confined to these flats. As this region is often many months without rain or dew, and the localities they select many miles from water, and the solid limestone which underlies the soil forbids deep excavations, it seems probable that they lived generally without water, or only such as the juices of the grass afforded them, and an examination of the stomach of one kill-ed by the sergeant confirms me in that opinion. Their general appearance is that of the squirrel family, though they are twice

---

27 For a time the Lewis and Clark description of the barking squirrel, as they called the prairie dog, was thought to be the first ever written. Bernard DeVoto (ed.), *The Journals of Lewis and Clark* (Boston: Houghton Mifflin Co., 1953), pp. 26, 28, 464.

Rio San Pedro Above the Second Crossing, 1857

By A. de Vaudricourt of the U.S. Boundary Survey, who accompanied Emory to the Devil's River, or Rio San Pedro.

From Vol. I of Emory's *United States and Mexican Boundary Survey.* Courtesy of Eugene C. Barker Texas History Center, University of Texas, Austin

FORT LANCASTER, TEXAS.—From a Sketch by a Government Draughtsman.—[See Page 182.]

Fort Lancaster, on the San Antonio—El Paso Mail Route

Located near the confluence of Live Oak Creek and the Pecos River. Stillman arrived here shortly after its establishment in August of 1855. This engraving from *Harper's Weekly*, March 23, 1861, shows development taken place in six years.

Courtesy of Eugene C. Barker Texas History Center, University of Texas, Austin

the size of the grey squirrel, and their tails not half the length
of their bodies. When they hear an unaccustomed sound they
will rear themselves upon their hind feet to see what it means,
and when they discover a white man approaching, with a gun
in his hand, they run to their burrows, and looking over the
little breast-work which is thrown up about them, they set up
the barking which has given them the name of prairie-dog, to
which the red squirrel of the North has just as much claim,
and whose bark, when you disturb him, very closely resembles
this marmot's. A small burrowing owl is common in these
towns, but what business it has there I could not learn. We
descended from these table lands into another wide valley,
several hundred feet deep, and camped near where there was a
little water standing in a "hole," in a rocky ravine. The feet of
the animals soon made it mud, but still they drank it. The
scenery here was very picturesque. A valley about a mile wide,
with a smooth, level floor, covered with grass and mesquets, here
reduced to a diminutive shrub, is shut in by the table lands
protruding in distinct heads, like hills, their flat tops on a level
with the general surface of the table lands, and all presenting
near the summits a perpendicular wall, like a parapet to a fort,
or the wall of an old castle, from which the earth sloped
abruptly down to the floor of the valley. From our camp that
night I counted eleven of these "Castle mountains," as they
have been called. The heavy strata of rock presenting themselves are uniform throughout, and were once continuous, but
the action of running water for ages has made this deep valley,
and separated their headlands a mile asunder. All the next day
we journeyed through this valley to where it opens into another
at Howard's Springs.[28] This is another noted camping-place. So
scarce is water in this region, for the most of the time, that any
party passing either way near it must stop here. The water rises
in considerable quantity through the pebbles in the bed of the

aroyo [*sic*], and disappears as suddenly. Even water-fowl are forced to resort to it, and in the muddy pond ducks are always to be found. It lies in the great Comanche trail[29] to Mexico, and is reputed to be a dangerous pass. A few small trees grow near the spring and a small thicket of willows grows in a ravine at the foot of a ledge of limestone, in the crevices of which juniper trees here called "cedars," begin to show themselves. I killed a turkey in the afternoon, and finding that they resorted to the willows to roost, I arranged with the sergeant that we should go at sundown to the bluff and shoot them as they came in. When I arrived at the spot there was a number of them in full sight, but as the sergeant had not come, I waited for him until it became so dark that I could scarcely see them. When he came, it was arranged that we should fire simultaneously, but one turkey only was killed, and we could no longer distinguish them in the obscurity of the night. Still we were disposed to hunt them, and we traversed the ravine, one on each side of the willows, until we could no longer distinguish each other. I had been stealing my way quietly along for some time without hearing anything from my friend, and I hailed him. When he exclaimed, close by me, "My God! Doctor, is that you! I thought it was a turkey!" He had indeed been following me for some time, trying to get a good sight at me, and my calling to him,

---

28 Howard's Springs probably is Howard's Creek that rises in southern Reagan County and flows thirty miles south through Crockett County to the Pecos in Val Verde County. See *Ibid.*, I, p. 855; *New Map of the State of Texas as it is in 1875* (N. Y: G. W. and C. B. Colton, 1874). Perhaps it is the stream that Lieutenant Whiting named Howard Lagoon, after Dick Howard, in 1849. "Journal of William Henry Chase Whiting," p. 255.

29 For decades the Comanches rode from areas as far north as Oklahoma to raid in Mexico and return with their booty. The trail crossed West Texas and entered the Big Bend country near Persimmon Gap. It split and formed an inverted "Y," with forks crossing the Rio Grande near San Carlos and Lajitas. Large amounts of stolen goods were carried back and forth over the trail. See Ralph A. Smith, "The Comanche Bridge Between Oklahoma and Mexico, 1843-1844," *Chronicles of Oklahoma,* XXXIX (Spring 1961), pp. 54-56.

perhaps saved me from the effects of a charge of slugs from his musket. The next day we travelled out of the valley and camped on the table land at the head of a cañon, whose depth we were prevented from seeing by the growth of cedars. The rain-water in rocks served our animals, and the grass was much better than we had seen for a week. In this vicinity, the prairie-dog towns are numerous and herds of the prong-horned antelope were seen.[30] They are very timid, and so difficult to shoot that their horns are rarely seen in the possession of any one but their natural owner. I arrived on the following day at the encampment where I now write, on Live-oak creek.[31]

J.D.B.S.

---

[30] Illustrated in A. B. Gray, *Survey of a Route for the Southern Pacific R.R., on the 32nd Parallel by A. B. Gray, for the Texas Western R.R. Company* (Cincinnati: Wrightson & Co.'s ["Railroad Record."] Print, 1856, reprinted in L. R. Bailey (ed.), *The A. B. Gray Report: Survey of a Route on the 32nd Parallel for the Texas Western Railroad, 1854, and Including the Reminiscences of Peter R. Brady Who Accompanied the Expedition* (Los Angeles: Westernlore Press, 1963), p. 16.

[31] Live Oak Creek, one of at least twenty streams in Texas to bear that name, flows from northwestern Crockett County fifteen miles southward to the Pecos. Webb, Carroll, and Branda (eds.), *Handbook of Texas*, II, p. 68.

The Crayon (New York), III (February 1856), pp. 40-43.

Wanderings in the Southwest
Second Series, No. 2

Camp Lancaster, Texas, *Oct.* 1855.

There is an extensive region of country lying west and north of the sources of the rivers of Western Texas, that will forever remain a desert—a region to be traversed by the caravan of the trader, wild winds, and wilder savages. Though subject to heavy rains, they generally occur at such long intervals that the roads through it have, of necessity, to be determined by the few localities which furnish a constant supply of good water.[1] The Camanches and Apaches rule it, and not a party travels through it that its strength and condition is not known by these matchless freebooters, while they manage to escape observation so completely that their presence is rarely suspected, until animals are lost, or one of the party is shot down by the arrow of an invisible foe, though their mode of warfare partakes much of the dashing chivalry of the Middle Ages, sometimes charging upon a superior force with lance and shield. As horsemen they are unrivaled; they sit very ungracefully, lolling about as they ride, as if drunk or too indolent to sit up; but, when roused to action, their energy is fearful. Their hideous yells—in making which they pass the hand rapidly over the mouth—and diabolical attire, are as appalling as the suddenness and fierceness of the attack. There is really little in them to command our admiration or respect: they rarely fight from any other motive than plunder or self-defence, and will never do the latter when there is a good chance to run, their tactics being

---

[1] Average yearly rainfall for this area from 1931 through 1960 was 25.30 inches. See *Texas Almanac and State Industrial Guide, 1970-1971* (Dallas: A. H. Belo Corp., 1969), p. 103.

those of attack and not of defence. They are very economical of their blood, esteeming the life of an Indian an equivalent for six white men, and no expedient unworthy a brave, whereby he may save his invaluable life, or any advantage too mean, in order to kill an adversary. In nothing is their sagacity more apparent than in the success with which they elude pursuit; it is rarely, if ever, that they are found when they are expecting pursuit; and that in a country so open as hardly to afford concealment. Major Simonson[2] cautioned me, when I left Fort Clark, to be always prepared for an attack, and I would see no Indians, and so it proved. Our mules were secured by strong chains to the wagon-tongues, so strong that, in case of an attempt to stampede them, their necks would break before the chains; and each soldier lay down near where his horse was picketed, with his gun at his side, and a vigilant watch was kept during the night.

To check the incursions of the Indians, the War Department establishes posts at the most important watering-places. The one at which I now write is near the junction of the "Live Oak Creek" with the Pecos, about eighty miles from where the latter empties into the Rio Grande.[3] The creek is about seven miles long, and affords a constant supply of clear, good water; on it are several groves of small live oaks; there are also a few gum-trees, and hackberries, willows, grape-vines, and rank weeds almost conceal the water, while they mark the course of the creek through a wide, deep valley. The Pecos rises in the mountains of New Mexico, north of Santa Fe, and flows

[2] Major John S. Simonson was a member of the Mounted Rifles when he met Stillman in 1855. Having joined the service as a Third Sergeant in 1841, Simonson served in the Mexican War before resigning in 1861. He later returned to the service and was given the rank of Brevet Brigadier General during the Civil War. Hamersly, *Register,* p. 759; Olmsted, *Journey Through Texas,* p. 285.

[3] Camp Lancaster was a federal post established in 1855 on the San Antonio-El Paso road, one half mile above the junction of Live Oak Creek and the Pecos River in Crockett County. Webb, Carroll, and Branda (eds.), *Handbook of Texas,* I, p. 627.

eight hundred miles without apparent increase. It is only about sixty yards wide; but its waters are deep, rapid, of a chocolate color, and saline taste. Its banks are bluff, and covered with rank grass, which nearly conceals its course; and, when riding through the valley, it is startling to find oneself for the first time upon the brink.

The valley of the Pecos is no less remarkable than the river itself. When approaching it on the table lands you see only an apparently unbounded, rolling plain, with occasional glimpses of deep gulfs or cañons on the left, until you find yourself upon the brink of a precipice among great masses of detached limestone, ready to tumble down by a little effort of your foot, down, crashing and bounding until they finally rest in a ravine, where thousands have fallen before. The valley is perhaps three or four miles wide, and bounded on the opposite side, as on this, by continuous walls of rock. As the eye wanders down the valley, it sees scarcely an object to arrest its attention. A thousand feet down, and off through the centre of the plain, the river pursues it[s] winding and mysterious course, invisible from the long, yellow grass, away to the south, until the blue of the rocky cliff is lost in the deeper blue of the distance. The engineers who, in 1849, surveyed this road to El Paso, were many weeks in finding a pass across this valley.[4] There are few places where a mule could descend directly from the table lands into this valley. Having gained the bottom, the scenery is picturesque, and not so barren as it appeared. A perpendicular wall of rock forms a bulwark around the summits of the

---

[4] The Topographical Engineers were instructed to survey West Texas in 1849 because Colonel John J. Abert, the commander of the Engineers, felt that a western road was essential to the maintenance of communications with the newly-acquired western territories of New Mexico, Arizona, and California. The Engineers, under Lieutenant Colonel Joseph E. Johnston, were to find a route for the road as well as explore the area. Averam B. Bender, *The March of Empire: Frontier Defense in the Southwest, 1848-1860* (Lawrence: Univ. of Kan. Press, 1952), p. 94.

whole amphitheatre of hills, composed of strata of great thickness, into which the caves, of which I spoke in my last, are excavated; from this bulwark an escarpment descends with greater or less abruptness to the floor of the valley, which again has a very gradual descent to the river. The valley is covered with low, thorny bushes, and grass intervening. One of the most remarkable features of this inhospitable region is the hostility with which every plant bears arms; some are entirely of thorns, compounded and decompounded, and so closely aggregated, that a sparrow could not build her nest in them. The Spanish bayonet, or Yucca, conspicuous and defiant, adds its many-pointed arguments why this is no country for a white man; and the trenchant briers of the Chaparral would strip him of his best defence, unless it were of buck-skin. Under foot is concealed, half-buried in the ground, and protruding with the grass, the venomous thorns of eight or nine species of Echinocacti. On the abrupt slopes, among the broken fragments of limestone and flints, a species of aloe spreads its thorny-pointed leaves just high enough to pierce the fetlock of a horse.[5] These grow more numerours [*sic*] the higher you ascend. The animal world is in keeping with the vegetable. Centipedes and millipedes, of extraordinary size, scorpions, tarantulas (*mygale*), one of which I have, which when living, spanned seven and a half inches, the vinagron, a repulsive crustaceous animal, about three inches long, with claws like a crab's, and whose odor is so strong when crushed, as to forbid its being killed in your tent, are all very common, and reported to be poisonous (?). There is a species of the true tarantula (*Lycosa*) found here, whose four eyes in a quadrangle, and each a line in diameter, glare upon you with the brilliancy of a wolf's in the dark. Add to these the rattlesnake, which you

---

[5] Many of these cacti are illustrated and described in George Engelmann, "Cactaceae of the Boundary," in Emory, *U. S. and Mexican Boundary Survey,* II, Pt. 2.

are liable to meet at any moment at your tent door and in your bed; the "horned frogs," and other saurians, spotted and striped, and you have a bill of fare around which Macbeth's witches might have "danced right merrily." Rich as this region is in insects and reptiles, it is poor in ornithology. Wild turkeys are abundant, and easily killed, as they are forced to resort to the few trees at night; and our best hunters often kill a half dozen on consecutive nights. Their food is despised by the Indians as enervating, hence the abundance of them in all those regions not frequented by white men. Two species of quail are common, but not abundant. The vulture hovers about the camp, and among them the croak of the raven is often heard. Sometimes a kingfisher may be seen sitting moodily upon a dry tree, over the water; a sparrow tilts away noiselessly from the bush before you; or a wren, busily engaged with her own domestic affairs, has no time to spend with you, and only stops to respectfully touch her tail to her head as you pass, and seems to wonder what so sensible a looking fellow can be doing in so desolate a country. Hawks are common, and they seem to have a hard time of it.

A few days since I was startled (for small things sometimes startle us in such a region) by hearing a great outcry among the captain's poultry in an adobe house just building in front of the tent where I was sitting; I ran to the spot where I expected to find a dog with one of the chickens, but in one corner of the roofless house, behind a log, was a hawk struggling with a rooster of twice his weight, his large yellow eyes glaring defiance and refusing to release his prisoner until I almost had him in my grasp; he then only retreated to a staging just out of reach, where he made a determined stand, and replied to the stones which I threw at him, by winks, until the captain returned with his gun and shot him. This month has witnessed the passage over us of great numbers of wild geese and ducks

on their way south; on one occasion I noticed that the five
first birds in the angle in which a flock were passing over our
heads were mallard ducks. This is a curious fact and shows
that these wild geese are veritable *geese* and not *know nothings,*
that they should be led off by an old drake and companions.
Blue and green winged teal visit the creek, and the avocet,
goosander, and some other migratory water-birds and waders
are sometimes seen; quadrapeds are still fewer. The black bear,
wolf, and fox, I have seen, as well as the great long eared
hare and small rabbit. The common deer of Texas, though not
so abundant as in the alluvial country below, are sufficiently
so, and the black-tailed deer of California are sometimes seen
on the table lands, with the antelope and marmot. A small
digitigrade herbivorous animal inhabits the holes in the cliffs,
but I could never see it, and there was no means of taking a
specimen. Decayed horns of the buffalo remind us that this
was once their range, but it is far to the north that the Indians
now hunt them. There is one drawback to hunting in this part
of Texas more serious than thorns or rocks—one never knows,
when he leaves camp to go any distance, but he may be made
game of himself before he returns.

> Up the airy mountain
> Down the rocky glen
> We daren't go a hunting
> For fear of little men.[6]

We never go to the creek to bathe, but our weapons are laid
upon the bank, so near that they may be reached at a moment's
notice. Such is the place where two companies of the 1st Infantry,
under Captain Carpenter,[7] are compelled to make themselves
as comfortable as possible for an indefinite period, and protect
themselves from Indians and ennui. As for any offensive opera-

---

[6] "The Fairies," by William Allingham. The only difference is that the original
verse reads, "Down the rushy glenn . . ." *The Oxford Dictionary of Quotations* (2nd
ed.; London: Oxford Univ. Press, 1966), p. 4.

tions, what can they do without horses, against these Arabs of the American desert? As well might dragoons be used as marines on the deck of a frigate. I have had every reason to be proud as an American of the character of our army officers; one never meets with a discourtesy from the graduates of West Point, or sees one that is not every inch a soldier, and it seems entirely out of place to send men to hunt Indians. It seems like a sad waste of science and talent. They are men worthy of a better foe. Their very energy is crippled by the necessity of conforming to orders, in so many ways, that they can accomplish nothing. The qualifications for this warfare are endurance, daring, cunning and coolness, and there should be entire freedom to conform to the necessities of the case, to hunt the Indian in his own style; to endure long marches without cooking, without baggage in silence; to hover about the track of the savage where ever it leads; to be a shadow to a shadow. What can be expected when an officer is sent with a company of riflemen, when they are sent with a long train of wagons, which can . . . barely carry forage for their own mules' consumption, thundering over the road, encumbered with hen coops and milch cows, tents, heavy-bedding and all the paraphernalia of the camps of a regular army, and their progress announced with a flourish of trumpets. Can we not laugh with the old warrior as he strips the flesh from the bones of a mule that he has stolen from the train the night before, and dries provision as he goes for a week's travel, and still follows the invader by the noise he makes as he goes. That these things are so, is not the other's fault, but he has to obey orders from the Secretary of War, who has never been in the country, and has no interest in bringing the war to an end. My travels in

7 Captain Stephen D. Carpenter was killed at the battle of Murfreesboro in 1862. He entered the service in 1840 and was promoted to Captain in 1851. Hamersly, *Register,* p. 346.

Texas have given me sympathy for the young officer who enters the service full of ambition for advancement and distinction, and finds himself an exile, banished, with all his new-born honors, to some frontier post, away from all the elevating influences of home. Long marches, hard labor, much danger, no honor, and great privations, and if by favor of his superior he is permitted to return to the haunts of civilized men, the savings of years are spent to defray the expenses of the journey. His recreations are few. Without his dog and gun what would he do? His West Point education has not opened to him the volume of nature in which he might find so much to instruct and amuse, his books are few, and in the dull routine of camp life he almost forgets whatever he knew. From reveille in the morning till tatto in the night, what has he done but obey orders? and during the lone night while he listens to the sentry's call, and the wolf's answer from the hill, what has he to think of but the chances of his promotion, or orders to some new post, which he hopes will at least afford him a change, if it does not improve his situation. He has no chances of distinction, and no hopes of promotion but in the death of his superiors. We are all very generous when we have nothing to give, and disinterested when we have nothing to gain; but if I were an officer in the army, where so much depends upon rank to which there is but one road, I do not know that I would not read the announcement of the demise of old Maj. Longwind, whereby I add a new bar to my shoulder-strap, with more unacknowledged satisfaction than I would of sorrow at the death of my junior officer.[8] Captain C., among his many good qualities, has that of a good sportsman, and in his two pointers, Cola and Quail, he finds the companionship that his long service on the frontiers has made congenial. Nor can I wonder at his attachment to them. Cola is finely developed, intellectually as well as physically; generally grave and uncommunicative to strangers, he goes into ecstasies at the prospect of a hunt, although in these adventures he generally comes back with a thorn in his foot; towards me, as his master's guest, he extends the rights of hospitality in the most cordial manner, and at the first sound of the drum that calls the garrison from their slumbers, Cola bounds through the tent curtains, and in the most impassioned manner, impresses upon my face the otherwise inexpressible joy he feels in seeing me so well; then seeing that his kindness is appreciated he disappears suddenly, before the order of our mutual congratulations has suffered from satiety. Quail, the junior dog, excels the other in the extravagance of the expressions of his regard, but I have not much confidence in the sincerity of his attachment; he makes too many friends in camp, and on several occasions I have detected him running away with one of my slippers. The steward said it was Quail that masticated my shoe-brush, and I strongly suspect him of stealing a bag of shot; at all events I charged him with it (the shot) upon which he barked twice, which, to say the least, was very equivocal, and he has discontinued his visits since. The readiness with which the dogs bark at night, on the approach of any unusual object, contributes more to the safety of individuals going about after dark than anything else. It is not an uncommon casualty to have a man shot through the body with

---

8 Quite another view of the army in Texas is represented by Joseph Wade Hampton, who wrote his wife in 1849 that, "The troops scatter among the people immense sums of money, and will keep plenty of it here so long as they remain; but they are a curse, morally and religiously, to any people among whom they may be located. The officers and men seem to fear God as little as if there existed no such being— most of them are avowed, and all I have seen, are practical infidels. Had I a son, I would rather close his eyes in death, than to place him in the army—and the naval service is no better. I regard the army and navy of the United States as only schools of infidelity, where young men have their minds poisoned, and are set in the road to ruin, if not for time, for eternity." Hampton was later editor of the *Texas State Gazette,* one of the most influential newspapers in Texas. Hampton to his wife, Austin, Dec. 19, 1849, in Joseph Wade Hampton Papers (Archives, Austin College Library, Sherman, Tex.).

an arrow in the dark, and even in the day-time, and yet no Indian be seen. Such was the fate of a musician to one of the companies now here, while it was encamped on Devil's River.

The command here is very busily engaged in preparing winter quarters, and as the Captain had expressed a desire to send out a party to explore a shorter route to Howard Springs, but could not spare an officer to go with it, I proposed to undertake it. I was furnished with three of the best hunters at the post, [Private Richard] Young, [Musician Thomas] Dennen, and [Private James] Beardall. We rode mules, and each man, besides his rifle, carried a six-shooter, a canteen of water, some biscuit, and a blanket. Descending the left bank of the Pecos about three miles, passing several cañons, we entered one that seemed most likely to furnish us the desired wagon-road; from its width, and the dry bed of a stream that bisected it, it would be called by the Mexicans an Aroyo [*sic*]. The cliffs on each side were not less than seven hundred feet above the ground on which we were riding, and everywhere impassable. As we advanced up this valley we saw other cañons entering to the right and left, each more narrow and impassable than the last. In the fissures of the rocks the cedars were growing, and the heads of the cañons were choked up with them. We continued on for two miles or more in the main valley, the passage of which grew each moment more difficult from the thickets, and rocks rolled down into the bottom. Beardall, who was riding a short distance ahead, motioned to us to keep back, and jumping from his mule he soon disappeared amongst the bushes. He had discovered some deer, high up on the rocky sides of the ravine, descending to the Pecos for water, and they came on in a file in confidence of entire security in this secluded ravine, where never the foot of white man had traveled before, until the report of Beardall's rifle startled the echos from the rocks, and send [*sic*] the deer bounding away, leaving a bloody trail.

The hunter followed the track until it led into another ravine. It soon became impossible to proceed, even for the surefooted mule, from the wild confusion with which the detached rocks, and dead and living cedars, were piled by the torrents after heavy rains. It had been apparent for some time that a wagon-road through this cañon was impossible, and we had been continuing on with the hope of finding a place where it was possible to get our animals out on the table lands, where we might continue our explorations at better advantage. Choosing a spot where the rocky wall seemed more broken down than elsewhere, we dismounted, and leading each his mule by the *cabris,* or strong rope by which they are secured, we succeeded in ascending several hundred feet over the loose rock and soil to the ramparts, to which I have already alluded. The difficulties of this part of the ascent were greater than we anticipated, but, by means of ropes and whips, we finally succeeded in getting our animals upon the plains. We then laid our course by compass to find other cañons lower down, which might furnish better facilities for a road, but they were all found to partake of the same characteristics. They are so peculiar and unlike those seen further east, that I would rather subject myself to the charge of being tedious than not to give a just idea of them. Their peculiarity depends upon the solidity of the uppermost stratum of the rock, which constitutes the whole mass of the earth. This stratum is of caen stone, and though soft, is fine in texture, and firm, while that immediately below is shelly; below these, the rock becomes harder and more crystalline, affording in some of them marble of fine qualities, and unique colors. When the rains have fallen, and the water has been seeking a passage from the table lands to the Pecos, it has glided over the surface until it reached the cliff where it has undermined the solid stratum above, and by the force acquired in its fall has cut away the harder rock below, thus forming these gulfs or cañons which, as they continue to extend into the table lands, divaricate like the ramifications of an artery, each ultimate branch terminating in a precipice. A hundred yards from the head they do not often exceed that width. There are no springs of water in them. Such luxuries occur only in the lowest places of the deepest valleys, and then but seldom.

Our progress was constantly interrupted by them; and we had no means of knowing our vicinity to them, until they yawned before us. Before we had gone far on the table lands, we found ourselves riding through a prairie-dog town, which I remembered to have seen on the day before my arrival at Camp Lancaster, and soon after came upon the road, when we saw a mail party bound to our post.[9] They were no less astonished to see us coming up from the cañons than we were to find we had cut off a day's journey.

We continued on to the south until three o'clock, without finding a spot where we dared attempt to descend with our mules, nor was I willing to risk it at the same place where we came up, as in the descent a single misstep would have been fatal. It was too late in the day to return by the same road, and it was determined to proceed at once to the cliff that overlooks the camp, and if we could not get our animals down, we could picket them for the night, and go down ourselves.

In passing the head of a cañon a fine buck started up from the bushes; and Young, leaving his mule, crept cautiously up to within a hundred yards, and fired. The deer fell dead in his tracks, and at the same time another sprang up from the grass, and, looking in bewilderment at his dead companion and in the direction whence the mysterious sound came, stood still

---

[9] The mail coach from San Antonio proceed to El Paso along two routes, one through Fredericksburg, Fort McKavett, and Fort Concho, the other through Fort Clark and Fort Lancaster. See Robert H. Thonhoff, *San Antonio Stage Lines, 1847-1881* (El Paso: Tex. Western Press, The Univ. of Tex. at El Paso, Southwestern Studies Monograph No. 29, 1971), endmap, fig. 14A.

while the hunter reloaded his rifle. The unwary victim fixed his attention upon me in the distance as having some connection with the alarm he had just received; his white breast exposed to full view, until another report from Young's rifle startled him. He ran a few paces, and again stood; the other hunters were now closing around him, and two shots were fired at him as he ran, but without effect; and I exploded a cap at him myself—the only time I have snapped a gun at a deer in Texas. Young's ball had passed through his lungs, and he was fain to lie down in the grass, with his face still to his foes and his horns erect, until Young again advanced and fired. One horn bounded to the distance of a rod as the ball struck the skull at its base, and at the same instant the head sunk forever in the grass.

"'Twas pitiful—'twas wondrous pitiful!" but the venison was excellent; and, having beheaded and disemboweled the two, they were packed behind Dennen and Beardall, and we hurried on. I have often visited the promontory overlooking our camp, and I thought it more easy of descent than any place I had seen during the day. The sun was setting, and we had no time to lose. A herd of antelopes bounded away, with their goat-like gallop, as we rode through the prairie-dog towns. It is not a little singular that the grass on the table lands is better than in the valleys, and clear from chaparral or agaves. Young and myself pushed forward, leaving the laden mules to follow, until, fearful that they would lose our trail, I directed Young to wait for them, and follow, while I made all the haste I could to reach the desired point before dark. Having found it, I returned to meet the men, and conduct them to it. Away across the valley the sky was still red when the sun went down, and threw a glare upon all the headlands, revealing the ravines and the canvas walls of our tents, like little white spots on the dark ground far below us. Our appearance on the cliff was at once discovered in camp, for our whole figures, mules and all, stood out in bold relief, upon the sky, and removed the anxiety of the commander, for a horse had been found in the vicinity of the post with an arrow shot into him, and the mail brought news of Indian outrages in the settlements; that the Rangers had invaded Mexico, and been repulsed; and that the settlers on the Leona and other places on the road to San Antonio, were being deserted from fear of invasion by the Mexicans and Indian[s] combined.[10] The prospect of my safe return through the hostile country seemed bad enough; but Major Ruff[11] was expected down in a few days with his company of mounted Rifles, on his return to San Antonio, from a reconnoissance in New Mexico, and with him I should feel safe.

A few days after the captain invited me to accompany him to the head of the creek to learn whether the grove of trees that grew there would furnish him a flag-staff, of which he stood in need. The sergeant brought me a mule to ride that was unaccustomed to the saddle, and the horn of the saddle was broken off, leaving a sharp and dangerous splinter in its place. When I was ready to mount the captain had already started on, and I had no time to change it, so, mounting in haste, I touched the mule with my spurs, when there ensued a series of evolutions not laid down in cavalry tactics, and entirely unbecoming the high position which for a moment I held. I was in a dilemma, of which the splintered horn before me gave the more serious apprehensions, when one movement, more vigorous than the rest, projected me, rifle, spurs and all, according

---

10 Indian raids in the area had been so frequent and devastating that settlers had petitioned Governor E. M. Pease to organize the militia for protection. The Mounted Riflemen had engaged Indians in several battles earlier in the year, and Texas Ranger Captain James H. Callahan had invaded Mexico in October. See Heitman, *Historical Register,* II, p. 401; Tyler, "The Callahan Expedition."

11 Major Charles F. Ruff had a long career in the army beginning in 1838. He participated in the Mexican War and the Civil War, resigning with the rank of Brevet Brigadier General. Hamersly, *Register,* pp. 734-35.

to the law of projectiles, into which my West Point friends had not duly indoctrinated me, over his ears, and I suspect over my own; but upon that point I had no positive impression, nor as to the point of contact with the ground. I only know that the spurs and myself, the principals in the affair, suffered no injury; and that the captain's invaluable rifle had its sights deranged, and the steward (my esquire) said that when he picked it off the ground it was more than half-cocked, for which unwarrantable calumny I ordered him to his quarters, and stopped his grog for the day. As to the mule, I judged his conduct to be perfectly justifiable, according to the laws of honor and the land. He did no more up to that moment than he was compelled to do, to maintain his self-respect. It was not necessary that he should continue to kick at me after I was down; but then his ears were so long that he could not help it. I concluded to permit the commander to get his own flag-staff, and repaired to my tent to write, and a considerable portion of this letter was written immediately after that event, so that, if it exhibits any special dullness, you must consider the long ears, and be as charitable as I.

It would seem impossible that a person could approach within view of our camp without being observed, for everywhere the high, undulating outlines of the cliffs affords scarcely a bush for concealment. I have seated myself for hours with a spy-glass, searching every object within its range, away for miles through the water-worn gorges of the long slopes, and into the cedar-choked cañons across the Pecos, where the whole hill-sides are in shadow soon after noon, but I could never distinguish a moving object, except our own animals grazing in the valley, and the gleam of the burnished musket of the sentry on a hill near them. There was one day a cry of "bear, bear," and those who were in readiness started for the cliff nearest camp with rifles and guns to run down the bear that had been seen running along the ledges near the summit. I joined in with others, and we had a grand hunt over the spurs of the hills, and into the cañons, and one or two joined us on horseback; but at length the information was sent after us that a soldier had seen a buzzard sailing along on such a steady and slow wing, just in range with the cliff, and had mistaken it for a bear, and we were all sold. This cliff is a favorite place of resort for me before sunset, not that the view is any wider than from the valley; but the effect of the setting sun as the shadows lengthen, and one eminence after another become involved in it, revealing ravines where none were ever seen before, and throwing those that were into bolder relief, until at length all below me became a homogeneous grey, and the cliff on which I stood still gilded, can be imagined, but to be felt must be seen. The stratifications of limestone on the slopes are but partially concealed by the thin soil and vegetation; and, as the captain remarked, on a visit he made with me to the place, the whole topography was mapped out below us by the lines of stratification, which to me resembled watered silk.

The abstract quality of vastness in this scenery awakens an emotion of sublimity in the mind of the most indifferent observer; but when to this is added the thought of the changes which it must have undergone, the successive deposits of such innumerable strata, of the debris of countless generations, of the same forms not only, but of the whole races of marine animals, whose vast marble monument has been raised from the depths of the sea to become the basis of a continent, and the water-worn furrows upon whose face, are deep enough to excite in us the emotion of sublimity, we feel like ephemera in the infinity of duration. I have observed that the emotions produced by vast mountains is not always in proportion to their vastness, but to qualities peculiar to different regions of the world. To one who stands upon Mount Washington, in New

Hampshire, and looks down upon the drifting clouds, and the "wide world dimly seen," surrounded by piles of misshapen lichen-covered rocks, where no insect or spire of grass lives, eternal *desolation* is the ruling idea, and it is overpowering. So, when I have stood upon a summit of the volcanic mountains of Peru or Central America, where the altitude was as great, and the desolation as complete; but where the vitrifices and sharp rocks, upon which not even lichens grew, seemed as if formed but yesterday, I am overwhelmed by the thought of the mysterious *power* that slumbered below me. I suppose that I am alluding to a fact that every lover of nature has felt, and one of a thousand that they only can.

J.D.B.S.

The Crayon (New York), III (March 1856), pp. 72-75.

Wanderings in the Southwest
Second Series, No. 3

Camp Lancaster, Texas, *Nov.* 1855.

On the morning of the 12th of October, I found Captain
Carpenter had made arrangements to go with a small party
to the head of Live Oak Creek, which he did not reach in the
previous effort, and I volunteered to accompany him, provided
I could find a horse worthy his rider. Mr. Savier, the sutler, had
a fine pony, almost an exact counterpart to my lost Pelicano of
pleasant memory, without his fear of firearms. "Pompey's nerves
are as solid as iron," Savier assured me, and his saddle was of
the best Texan manufacture, and nearly new. It was charming
to be so well mounted, and I hurried up to join the Captain.
With us were Beardall, Dennen, [Private Patrick] M'Culloch,
and a teamster driving a six-mule team, to bring the poles that
were to be cut. The Captain rode his favorite old blood-horse,
"Driver," and was accompanied by his two dogs. His "six-
shooter" hung at the horn of the saddle, and across the saddle
in front of him he carried his shot-gun. Over one shoulder
hung his powder-flask, and at the other his shot-belt; an ivory
whistle, fashioned after a dog's head, was suspended at a button-
hole of his hunting-jacket. Beardall was armed simply with a
rifle, and rode a bare-boned, black pony, in which everything
seemed wanting but the essential *go*. Dennen rode a horse also,
and was armed with a double-barreled gun, and into his pocket
he had slipped a few musket-cartridges, each containing an
ounce ball, and four buck-shot. M'Culloch had his musket and
cartridge-box, and rode with the teamster, who was unarmed.
The distance to the source of the creek was not more than
seven miles for mounted men, and a mile further for the team,

but we were all to meet at the crossing of the creek, three miles distant, from which point there was no road. We four who were mounted rode up the valley on the south side of the creek. The Captain and Dennen kept close up under the hill, on a military reconnoisance [*sic*]. Beardall skirted the creek, in hopes of falling in with game, while I held on *in medias res,* ready for anything that might turn up, with a shot-gun and No. 6 shot, the best I had since Quail ran off with the larger size. My attention is arrested by a pile of small stones to the amount of several tons, resembling that which is broken up for macadamizing a road. Was it the grave of an Indian? I could not tell. I would have explored it, but it was the work of several men for half a day, and I rode on. When I joined Beardall I mentioned it, and he told me he had seen similar ones, but did not believe they were graves, as there were some undoubted graves near where we were going, and they were very unlike these. We hunted along the creek for ducks, and never before did we look so far in vain. Crossing the creek where the El Paso road crosses it, we all met on the north side, and continued on, keeping close to the creek, where a belt of coarse grass intervened between it and the chaparral, in order to avoid the thorns of the latter, no less than the ravines that intersected the plains. The creek is almost concealed by the growth of small trees and grape vines, whose leaves, already fallen, rustled under our horses' feet. We cross a deep ravine, where the bank of the creek is high and free from thickets, and a sandbar makes out from the ravine, meeting the bare rock on the other side, and over which the creek glides with little noise. A chaparral cock (*Geocoxyx mexicanus*), the first I have seen since I left Fort Clark, ran across, and disappeared on the other side.[1] On each side of the valley, opposite to each other, and a mile

---

[1] Illustrated in Cassin, *Birds of California, Texas, Oregon, British and Russian America,* plate 36.

asunder, are two natural curiosities, which I noticed when I first descended the creek, as they are distinguishable at a great distance. Were we not in a region where castle-crowned hills were always in sight, one would pronounce these two to be artificial works. They are completely isolated, and their tops apparently inaccessible without ladders, rounded, and one third way down the escarpment; that on the north side has another circular wall, as an outwork; that on the south has four disconnected outworks, forming a square around the hill, flanking each other, and commanded by the castle above them. As *lusi naturae,* they are wonderful. Having reached the grove, which is ten or more acres in extent, the team was left outside, while the Captain, with three men, proceeded to open a way through the dense weeds and undergrowth that rendered the thicket impenetrable to the eye. The creek intervened, and was nearly obscured by the rank growth of weeds and flags—from which a flock of turkeys took wing and flew around the mott. I continued on alone, along the little chain of ponds which formed the sources or springs of the creek, until there appeared only a dry aroyo, and a treeless valley, stretching away to the northwest, until it was lost in the haze of the distance. I returned to rejoin the party, whom I found hard at work in the heart of the mott, cutting trees. The live oaks were too crooked to serve their purpose, but some hackberry and gum-trees furnished poles comparatively straight for the distance of thirty feet. Leaving the four men at work, the Captain and myself passed out on the other side of the grove, with the intention of going to another and smaller mott of trees, half a mile further up, and to the right of the aroyo, where the turkeys were supposed to have fled. I stopped to examine a shrub which bore a strong resemblance to the apple-tree; the leaves were all fallen from it, and I could not be certain, but I believe it to belong to that genus. As I remounted, the Captain was just disappearing around the edge of the wood. The grass was very long and coarse, such as is used for thatching, and patches of dead weeds almost buried my horse. I found Driver tied in a little opening on the left of the grove, and there I tied Pompey, well concealed, and plunged into the thicket, as I heard the report of the Captain's gun, to get my chance at the game. This grove was entirely of small live oaks, with much undergrowth. There was an abundance of turkey signs in the deepest shade, where the ground was bare; they had nestled in the dirt during the heat of the day, digesting their morning's feast of acorns, and filling their feathers with dust. I proceeded cautiously, expecting each moment to get sight of a file of red heads stealing through the bushes, (for even when full-grown, the wild turkeys follow their parents in Indian file) until I had traversed the thicket. The Captain was not there. Where could he be, and what meant the report of a gun? At the edge of the wood, opposite that at which we had entered, I was startled by the sight of a trail of four or five horses. No party from our camp had ever been here, and white men from any other quarter were still less likely to have been. They entered from above. I inspected the trail closely; it could not have been more than two days old, for the tracks were sharp, though dry to dustiness. It could not have been made by wild horses, or strayed ones, for such avoid thickets, and the tracks were so deep as to make it certain that they had riders; besides, I noticed that it did not pass under the branches, but around them. The Indian horses are unshod, or only with raw hide when necessary; only one of these was shod, and he must have been recently stolen. What had these tracks to do with the shot I heard, and the absence of the Captain? I thought I would follow the trail until I should find that of the Captain. I dared not call, and I crept along carefully avoiding breaking twigs, or making noise that might betray me. I soon heard something rushing towards [*sic*] me, breaking and bearing down the bushes, and my breath grew rapid as I raised and cocked my gun, for though I had but fine shot, the bushes were so dense, that when the object became visible, the shot would be as effective as ball. I saw the two white dogs of the Captain, and their master's legs, and hailed, "Captain, what's the matter?" although my mind naturally connected what I had already discovered with the Captain's alarm. "Where are the horses?" "This way," said I, and led off in quick time in the direction where, to the best of my recollection, the animals were concealed. Having found them and mounted, "Now, then," said he, "I have old Driver and the six-shooter, let them come on." "Where are they, Captain?" He then explained, as we rode back to join our party, how he had wounded a turkey, and pursued it over the hill with his dogs in full chase, when, just as he reached the crest, he saw a large party of Indians at the foot of the opposite slope. He called in his dogs at once, and thought they must have been observed, and started to return for his horse, but taking a second thought, he returned to reconnoitre. There were fifteen up in a file, and several others riding up in the line. To the best of his judgment there were nineteen, well mounted, armed with shields, bows and arrows, lances, and a few guns; they were painted and bedevilled for war. The hill to which he referred was a long, narrow ridge, running parallel to the creek, and about fifty feet high. It commenced just above the crossing, and above the motts it turned off to the right gradually, and terminated in the high bluffs. Having returned to the thicket where the men were at work, the Captain ordered that no one should leave the spot for hunting or other purposes, but that all haste should be made to complete the loading of the team, and we rode down the creek, with the view of crossing it and the hill in rear of the savages, to inspect their trail, and to keep an observation upon them. We had

gone a few hundred yards, when the report of a gun in the mott caused us to return. Beardall had fired his rifle in order to light his pipe, and the Captain was now unwilling to leave the working party until we could all leave together. We all fell to work to expedite matters, so as to get out of the way of the Indians, and permit them to go up the valley unobserved, as they seemed disposed to do. The skirts of the thicket were so dense that we could not see out, and if they designed mischief, they knew better than to attack us there. There was no doubt that they intended to escape observation, and were bound up the country.

The wagon being loaded, was driven out into the level ground, where the flag-staff had been previously dragged, and this was still to be adjusted to the load; and, as the Captain was not there to direct, much time was lost. Growing impatient, I went back to find him. He was concealed in the skirts of the further end of the mott, watching the hill over which he had seen the Indians, and where they must pass to reach us. The presence of our chief having adjusted difficulties, we were soon on our way, in the order in which we came. As the Captain was still anxious to reconnoitre, he took Beardall with us, and we proceeded in advance, leaving Dennen and McCulloch to go with the team. From the tangled thickets of grape-vines, buckeye, and other shrubs, that choked the ravine of the creek, it was difficult to find a passage across it. The long hill here came down close to the creek, and the bank was abrupt. "Here," said Beardall, "on the highest part of this hill, are those Indian graves of which I spoke." We determined, if possible, to take these in our course. The team being delayed, we waited a short time, until the Captain returned with Beardall, to aid them, if necessary, and I lost sight of them as well as the team from the inequality of the ground.

I stood still while Pompey browsed the coarse grass. The sun

was about three hours high, and the eastern slopes of the hills
were already in deep shadow. One feels in such a country a
constant disposition to gaze even when the uniform glare of
the sun on the rocks, and the distance to which one looks,
make the act painful to the eyes; for the fewer objects of
interest there are, the more we look for them. From the bend
in the long hill, which had been the object of so much solic-
itude, and the small elevation of the part opposite to me, I
could, from my position, get a rear view of the part where the
Indians had been seen. The little valley where they were was
bounded on every other side by impassable bluffs, and the
conviction forced itself upon me that the savages were there
for no other object than concealment. At the same moment a
yell from the direction of our party drew my attention, and a
scene burst upon me that nearly paralyzed my nerves. The
incarnate fiends! Running to and fro with the swiftness of
hell-hounds and yells of triumph over the very spot where I
had just before seen my companions! I saw the teamster running for his life towards the creek, and two nearly naked and
painted, mop-[h]aired savages in close pursuit, and making
two yards to his one; the white man disappeared, and I saw
only the infuriated savages. I strained my eyes to see if any
one had escaped from the *mêlée;* but there was not one, and
my turn was next. The two savages who had run down the
teamster came towards me like blood-hounds, without a sound,
as though their object was not to alarm me, but to kill. I had
not heard a shot fired. Had the surprise been so complete!
There was no time for reflections. A warrior, mounted on a
pie-bald horse, joined the runners, and I had no doubt that
they would all be down upon me as soon as they could mount
their horses. Turning Pompey's head towards camp, and striking him with shot-gun and spurs at the same moment, I soon
put his mettle to the test, as well as my own equestrianship.

He vaulted over the chaparral with the elasticity of the Spring-bok, clearing a rod at a bound. It was my first lesson in the steeple-chase, and I did not know but each bound would be the last. I would have dropped the gun, but it was not mine, and it served me for a whip, and might yet save my life, should the enemy close upon me; and on I went, holding on with one hand to the horn of the saddle, and the other to the gun. The deep ravine which we noticed coming up yawned an instant before me, and the next we were poised on the opposite brink; here my horse voluntarily stopped, as though he was sprung, and until then I could not look back without great risk of being thrown. I could not tell, from the inequality of the ground and the shrubs that intervened, whether the pursuit was continued. I knew that Pompey was good for them, pro-vided we could keep together; but I feared that a party might, by following the creek out of my sight, still cut me off in my fancied security, and I gave Pompey the reins. I had yet three miles to run through the chaparral before I could strike the El Ross[2] road that led past the camp. A herd of deer broke before me, as if they thought I was after them, and for a time held on my way, but soon fell off to the right and left, to let me pass. I discovered that my horse was running away, and paid no attention to the bridle, but would use his own discre-tion whether he would jump a bush or go round it, and in the effort to manage him the bridle parted in my hand; but, as he held on towards camp, I had only to hold on to him.

Once more on the road, I felt that I had a good chance of living to fight another day, and I quietly resolved that the first requisite for that purpose was a good horse. My arrival at camp, swaying in my saddle from exhaustion, and the appear-ance of the horse told all that I could. I reported the whole

2 Perhaps this should be El Paso road.

party killed, as I had no doubt they were, before I "broke" for camp. The probable death of Captain Carpenter, who was so much beloved by the whole command, created a most painful sensation. There was a hurrying of men to arms, and a party started off on foot at quick time. In the meantime, a large draft of whiskey and water, and a portion of cold turkey, which had been waiting for me, so far revived me, that I was ready, with a fresh horse, to accompany Lieuts. Reynolds[3] and Williams[4]; but Savier, whose horse I had, claimed the privilege of riding it himself. When they were gone, I climbed the hill in the rear of the camp, to watch their progress. It was just dusk when I saw the Captain, to my great surprise as well as delight, slowly riding in, and I ran down to meet him. He supported a bloody hand, his horse was bleeding and an artery in the fore-leg cut, and his dogs, at his horse's heels, were of a crimson color from head to foot. The sight was sanguinary indeed. McCulloch followed on foot, limping with an arrow-wound in the foot.

"Is it possible, Captain, that you have escaped?" He held out his hand to me, and asked if he was badly hurt. I examined the wound, and assured him that he was not. "The rascals were determined to have old Driver," said he; "but I was determined they should not, while I could defend him." At the camp I proposed to dress the Captain's wound, but he told me to save Driver if I could. An arrow had transfixed his leg and severed an artery, and his life was fast ebbing from the wound. A compress and bandage arrested the blood, and he was led down to the correll [*sic*], with instructions to the Orderly to give him all the water he would drink. While I was

---

[3] Lieutenant Samuel H. Reynolds was a veteran of six years service in the army when he met Stillman. He resigned his commission when the Civil War started. Hamersly, *Register,* p. 717.

[4] Lieutenant George A. Williams joined the army in 1852. He fought gallantly during the Civil War and retired in 1870 with the rank of Major. *Ibid.,* p. 863.

dressing the Captain's hand, through which an arrow had passed, he told me the particulars of the attack.

At the moment in which he reached the team, which had stopped to adjust the loading, he saw the Indians issuing from the wood directly on our tracks, and approaching to within two hundred yards, open to the right and left, to encircle the little band. Their intention was to *stampede* the party, according to their custom, run down the fugitives, and take their scalps and horses. But they had an extraordinary man to deal with. Captain C. immediately dismounted, as did Dennen and Beardall, and gave orders not to fire, until the savages should approach so near as to make a sure thing of each shot. Several rifleshots were fired by the Indians at too long range to do any execution, but by which they hoped to draw the fire of our men, when they would have charged in upon them, and despatched them before they could reload. Disappointed in this, they withdrew a short distance, when our men started on with the mule team, but the Indians, having secured their animals, now returned to the attack on foot. The teamster, being unarmed, acted on the advice of Beardall, and abandoned his team, and fled for safety to the creek, unconsciously followed by the two savages, who I supposed had killed him. The position of the Captain was in the grass, which skirted the creek a few rods wide; beyond this the ground rose somewhat, and was covered with the thin, scattered bushes of which I have already spoken.

The Indians approached under cover of the bushes, rising to let fly an arrow, and immediately hiding again, before a sight could be drawn upon them, and all the while they were in sight, jumping about in the most sprawling and ungraceful attitudes, at the same time yelling, to frighten the men from their steadiness of aim. Our men dodged the arrows successfully, until the Indians approached within fifty yards, when they began to return the fire.

Dennen and Beardall were musicians to Company K, and from boyhood had served in the army of the frontiers, were expert hunters, and cool as if it were only deer that they had to shoot. Beardall felt the brush of an arrow, and saw the Indian who shot it, and disregarding all others, he held his rifle to the spot where he saw him disappear behind a bush, until he rose again, when he fired, and the savage fell without sending his arrow. There seemed to be two Indians who were decorated with whistles, and which they used to stimulate their men to the attack, as they singled out the Captain as particularly worthy of their regard. One of them was a huge-framed fellow, whose vermillion-colored face bore more malignity than he had ever seen expressed in a human countenance. They advanced upon him at right angles, launching their arrows from behind their circular shields. The Captain held his horse and shot-gun by the left hand, and in his right his six-shooter, pointing the latter at the chiefs alternately. He had already fired three shots, and his antagonists had advanced to twelve paces from him. One arrow had struck his horse, which was rearing and plunging, one severed the strap at his shoulder, which held his shot-belt, another transfixed his boot from behind, passing between the sock and his leg; this he drew out with his other foot; a fourth pierced his heavily-quilted hunting-coat, and passed through, and a fifth struck his hand in which he held his gun, by which the force of the arrow was arrested from passing into his vitals. It was a critical moment for him. He had abandoned all hope of saving his own life, and became intent only on selling it dearly. If his next shot failed he was lost; he levelled his pistol upon the fierce chief in front of him, who stopped, the more perfectly to protect his body with his shield, when, by a quick movement of the pistol, he brought it to cover the other chief, who was closing upon him with his spear, and struck him full in the chest before he could raise his shield. Then, dropping his pistol, he was about to try the effect of the shot in his gun upon the shield of the other chief, but he was already stretched out dead, in all his ferocity and paint. A cartridge from Dennen's gun laid him low, just at the moment that he was about to spring upon the Captain. It was the work of a moment; and all was as hushed about them as a calm after a storm. The whistle no longer sounded to the charge, and our men stood ready to meet another attack; but, save the gurgling breath of the dying chiefs, not an indication was given of their being in the vicinity.

The mule-team, during the fight, had strayed off, grazing, amongst the bushes, to the distance of several hundred yards, when an Indian rose from his concealment and led them off up the valley; and the Captain felt himself in no condition to make an effort for their recovery. Beardall's horse, which he had hitched to the wagon, in order that he might drive the team, after the flight of the teamster, fell also into their hands. From the concealment afforded by the bushes, it was impossible to tell the extent of their loss, and reinforcements did not arrive on the ground until an hour after the Captain left it, and the Indians had carried off their dead and wounded, according to their custom. They knew that I had escaped to camp, and that reinforcements would soon be at hand, and they lost no time in getting away. Lieutenant Reynolds found one of the mules still hitched to the wagon, and an arrow sticking in his side, but he was not seriously injured by it. Pieces of harness were scattered along the trail. A small bear-skin, wet with blood, and several articles of Indian wearing-apparel, and arrows, were strewn about the ground where the conflict took place.

These Indians were a band of Apaches, and, as we learned by following their trail afterward, they had observed us in the morning as we passed up the creek, from their concealment in one of the cañons near the north fort; and they descended and crossed the valley, keeping themselves concealed in the bottom of the ravine, from which, seated on their horses, they could just observe our movements; and when we entered the mott, they crossed the creek and passed along under the hill to where they were seen by the Captain at noon. There they waited until our full number had left the grove and were on open ground, where there was no chance of escape. Their dispositions were well made, and the whole plan of attack showed great sagacity, and would have been successful in cutting off every man in the party, were it not that they wanted victory too cheap. They are not satisfied to get victory, unless it can be had for nothing. But, the fact is, that, in a great majority of cases, they would have been left in possession of the field under the circumstances.[5] Two days after this affair, a train of wagons, bound for Fort Davis,[6] which, had left our camp but a few days before, was surprised by a large party of Indians, and every animal was carried off, amounting to sixty-six, in broad daylight—the men not firing a shot in their defence. This was my first sight of an Indian in Texas, although I had had such convincing evidence that they had more than one of me. I shall be glad to know that it will be the last. I had rather die by wild beasts, than by the hands of beings who possess all the ferocity of the wildests beasts, added to the cunning and cruelty of man.

I had promised to my friend Dr. Nott, of Mobile, a skull of this tribe, if I could get it; but I think I would prefer to send him mine, while it is at my disposal, than to pursue such ethnological inquiries of such risks.

The next morning two parties were sent out, under Lieutenants Reynolds and Williams, one to the crossing of the Pecos,

---

[5] This is the fight reported in the *San Antonio Zeitung*, Nov. 3, 1855, p. 2, col 5, and *The Galveston Weekly News*, Nov. 13, 1855, p. 1, col. 9.

[6] Founded in 1854, Fort Davis was to protect the western road. At first it was called Painted Comanche Camp. Webb, Carroll, and Branda (eds.), *Handbook of Texas*, I, pp. 623-24.

and the other to follow the trail. But the parties being on foot, and a drizzling rain having fallen during the night, making the walking very laborious, the pursuit was abandoned. This was the first rain that I had seen in two months; during all that time the sky has been almost, if not quite cloudless. A northerly wind has occasionally broken the monotony of fine weather, and rattled our tent-ropes and stiffened the locusts that came in myriads with the first north wind, and made another blanket comfortable at night. In a few days I shall be again upon the road to leave a dreary country and a pleasant camp, where I have experienced many kindnesses and cordial greetings, that one will look for in a band among the crowded "tents of Israel."

J.D.B.S.

The Crayon (New York), III (April 1856), pp. 105-07.

Wanderings in the Southwest
Second Series, No. 4

On the morning of the 27th of October, an unusual stir amongst the camp dogs announced the arrival of a stranger at the Post, and in a few moments a tall hunter rode up, dressed in buck-skin breeches and frock-coat. His name was Clowd; he was guide to Major R.,[1] and he announced the arrival of the long-expected company of mounted Rifles, commanded by that officer; they were returning from a long search for Indians, with but trifling success, and I purposed to avail myself of this opportunity to return to San Antonio. Soon after, a squadron of horsemen appeared over a low hill, where the winding of the El Paso road loses itself to our view; a long train of wagons followed, their white covers shining in the sun, and successively disappearing in the ravine. Their first camping-ground was to be seventeen miles distant, and I had no opportunity to reach the team with my baggage, unless a team was sent expressly to overtake them. Several hours passed before I could get it in readiness, and an escort of six men was sent with me; for all of which I am indebted to the kindness of Captain Carpenter, by which he added another to the many claims he has to my grateful remembrance. A hurried farewell to my late companions, and to my fast friends, Cola and Quail, and I was bounding over the rocky ground, away from the scenes that I shall never see again, though every feature of them is indelibly stamped upon my recollection. We had a distant view of the theatre of our late conflict with the Apaches, passed up through the cañons, and out again upon the table-lands, and among the dog-towns, at a rapid rate, but could not overtake the Rifles,

---

[1] Major Charles Frederick Ruff. See note 11, chapter 9.

until they had nearly reached their camp. I found Major R. an invalid, carried in an ambulance, and he tendered me his horse to ride.

The Major and Assistant-Surgeon Smith[2] were the only commissioned officers in the command, and I was provided for in the Doctor's tent. Whiskey seems to be regarded as an essential in the stores of a campaigner; and the Captain, some days before my departure from Camp Lancaster, had placed a bottle of choice quality in mine, which I produced and presented to the mess, with a high encomium upon its quality. The Major prepared from it, with elaborate skill, a choice toddy; and, upon tasting it, declared that he did not appreciate the quality of the liquor. I took up the bottle, it looked paler than it ought; I tasted it, and the truth flashed upon me, that my servant at the Post had taken advantage of my delay in getting off, and substituted water for the greater part of my whiskey. "I beg your pardon, Major; but I believe some one has substituted water in the bottle." "Yes," said he, gruffly, tasting it again, "and *d—n bad water, too!*"

Before daylight the next morning, the bugles sounded the *reveille,* and the camp was soon all astir. A hundred and fifty mules were to [be] harnessed, and fifty horses to be groomed and fed, while fires were lighted in all directions, preparatory to breakfast: a fatigue-party strike[s] the tents, and stow[s] the wagons and the teamsters begin the day's work of beating and damning the mules. Breakfast over, the call of "boots and saddles" increases the commotion, and all are soon in readiness to start, when the bugles "sound to horse," and before its last note is ended every man is mounted, and another day's march begins. The Major leads off in his ambulance, followed by his boy, like

---

2 Assistant Surgeon Andrew K. Smith was appointed First Lieutenant in 1853. From Connecticut, he later served with the Union army and was promoted to Brevet Colonel in 1865. Hamersly, *Register,* p. 764.

a dark shadow that he is, on a pony, his legs being too short to reach the stirrups, his feet rest in the straps. Next ride the Surgeon and the "Wanderer," smoking remarkably long pipes; then comes a wagon with camp equipage and baggage of the officers, behind it hangs a hen-coop, whose inmates are expected to lay eggs at every favorable opportunity, in default of which they are liable to get into a stew. Next come the company of riflemen, under the immediate command of the First Sergeant, and preceded by two men with bugles slung at their backs. The mornings are foggy, for it is late in October, and the nights are cool. About nine o'clock the sun breaks out; overcoats are laid across the saddles, and still it grows hotter. We become thirsty, and drink from a canteen that hangs at the horn of the saddle; the water is warm, and how could we "take it cool." Ye gods! what a thing it is to be a soldier, and wear a little cap with not enough of front to protect the nose from blistering; to be a soldier and serve one's country brown. But the wagons string so far behind, that I had almost forgotten them, and the rear-guard I never saw on the march. Arrived at Howard's springs, a halt is made of a couple hours, in order to afford an opportunity for the animals to get water, for we camp that night where there is none. Hastily unsaddling and turning my horse loose, I hurry down to the water to get a good draught at a small spring, that in my way up I had cleaned out and walled up, for those that might come after me; but, to my surprise, it was filled up with water-plants and insects that feed upon them, so I put my face down at the edge of the pond where there was a space clear from weeds, and drank my fill with the rest. There were no ducks in the pond, so I took my gun and strolled up the ravine, where I had killed turkeys a few months before; but the leaves were fallen from the willows, the buck-eye bushes and the grape-vines, and the turkeys had grown older and wiser. Here was the first opportunity that I had had to realize that autumn is here also, as well as in the far regions of the north—a desolating season, and even when there is no killing frost, there too "leaves have their time to fall, and flowers to wither." A large "prairie snake" lay coiled up in my path, with its head resting close by a marmot's hole, apparently waiting for him to make his exit, and seemed not at all disposed to leave on my account. From my earliest recollections I have regarded it a virtue to kill a snake, and my aversion to that class of animals has in no wise diminished since I have learned to call them by their more respectable cognomen of Ophidian reptiles—are they not still serpents, and am I not of the seed of woman? My gun was loaded with small shot in one barrel and buck-shot in the other; but I was unwilling to make a noise by firing it. I thought I could crush his head with the breech of the gun, but I was mistaken. I held him with it, however, until I could place my foot upon his neck, and draw-out the ramrod; while his majesto took a turn around my leg, I endeavored to screw the wormer of the rod into his head, but the skull was too thick, and I grew desperate; notwithstanding my whole weight was upon him, he was slipping out from under my foot, and, so to decide the matter, I placed the muzzle of the gun to his head and fired. This was the largest snake I had seen in Texas, and measured three feet longer than my gun. It is not a venomous species; but they are more often met with in the open country than any other, except the rattle-snake. They are very destructive to poultry in the new settlements, and I killed one a few days after on the San Fillippe, [*sic*] attempting to swallow a rabbit. Our camp for the night was chosen in a valley, where it was so dark, that it was difficult to select our ground. The grass was rank and dry, and as our fires were kindled they spread amongst it, and were allowed to burn far enough to prevent their rekindling in the night, and then extinguished by beating the flames with empty

corn-sacks, for the want of bushes. In a box, which was taken
each night from the wagons and placed in the tent, was a jar
containing all the small reptiles that I could collect during my
stay at Camp Lancaster. Among them were scorpions, tarantulas, lizards, centipedes, snakes, etc., and the jar was filled
with whisky for their preservation. I noticed that this bottle
was out of the place into which it had been closely fitted, and
upon examining it, it appeared that one of the men who had
taken it from the wagon, smelling the coveted beverage, and it
being too dark to see the contents, had drank off a half pint of
the tincture, and was unable to replace the jar. As the party
who unloaded the wagon would be the same on duty in the
morning, it was left out for the benefit of the man, if he would
relish the same by daylight. The affair was soon rumored
through camp, but the offender was not discovered. Our guide,
Clowd, whom we had not seen during the day, came into
camp with a fine buck lashed to his saddle. He is a remarkable
man; he leaves camp in the morning before the train, and we
see him no more till we make our next encampment, when
we generally find him with some game that he has killed during the day. He evades the society of all but one companion,
with whom he seems never to speak. He is said to be a native
of Tennessee; his appearance is that of a man of great intellect
and perfect physical development; he knows the wilderness
like a book, and he has that important accomplishment possessed by few even on the frontiers—of a good hunter. This is an
art of more difficult attainment than is generally supposed by
those who do not know the habits of game. I have had experience enough to convince me that one may perish from hunger
in the midst of game, from the want of skill in hunting it. One
should never rely upon it exclusively who travels in the most
favored regions in that respect.

The next day we reached the Devil's river, and stopped at

an old camp-ground which was covered with the feathers of wild turkeys that had been slaughtered here. There was a pond of water near by, but the head of the stream was yet ten miles below. My bad success as a hunter did not deter me from another trial at the turkeys. I repaired to the deepest part of the thicket, where a large button-wood tree (sycamore) threw its branches far over the water, and around which were abundant signs of turkeys. Concealing myself in the roots of an upturned tree, I waited patiently for two hours, until it was almost dark, when the intrusion of a couple of riflemen dissipated my hopes of roast turkey. It was strange that they would not come back to roost there, such a secluded place as it was, and so perfectly safe. Clowd came in soon after with eight that he had killed with his rifle, and he said that the ninth had escaped him. It was delightful to find one's self once more in the wooded bottoms of this river, amongst the pecans and live oaks, through which we journeyed the next day, and camped on the bank of the river where the road leaves it for the high lands again. It was early in the afternoon, and after bathing in the limpid water, we gathered pecans, which were very abundant, notwithstanding the large number of turkeys, wild hogs (*Peccaries*), and bears that subsist upon them. They were so abundant that in an hour I gathered a half bushel, but in the deep shadow of the trees the poison-oak (*Rhus toxicodendron*) covers the ground, and notwithstanding the lateness of the season, and its leaves were livid red with their approaching fall, I was again severely poisoned. The scene at this crossing is the most picturesque that I had seen on the route. A broad sheet of blue water surrounded by the dark green foliage of the oaks overarching the road, and the cliffs of limestone beyond, above, and surrounding all, and shutting out the winds, and the beams of the declining sun, conspired to throw a spell of wild beauty about the place, that caused me to sit there until the sober

shadows of night gathered upon it all. Darkness found me there, seated alone upon a rock, with my feet in the water, listening to its music among the stones below, and wondering why the Mocking-bird, the Cardinal, and all the tuneful train of birds had left it for other regions. Their departure more than anything else, reminded me that another autumn with its yellow melancholy was at hand, another season of vegetable repose. That night was very dark, and I was roused from a sound sleep by the Doctor, who said the Indians were stampeding the animals. I could hear a great commotion in camp —the hailing of the sentries, and the mules jerking at their chains, but I comforted myself with the consciousness that I had no horse more to be stolen, and I had no relish for having a wooden skewer run through my vitals without some adequate consideration—and I was lying not far from the grave of a man who was killed a year before, by his fellow traveller mistaking him in the dark for a Comanche. Quiet was soon restored, when it was found that a stray mule had been loafing about the camp, and had alarmed the other animals. The next two nights were spent on the table-lands, where water was found only in holes, and stagnant. The rear guard came into camp one night with a bear that they had killed near one of these water-holes after we had left it. A ham from it was sent to our mess, but its meat was so poor and tough, that it was impossible to eat it.

A journey through the wilderness, over a road that you have travelled before, even with the luxury of a good horse, and entertaining companions, is fatiguing, and one hears the order to halt with more interest than any other word during the day; and there is a longing for the end, when the travel-worn again rest under the friendly shadow of a roof: I looked, therefore, with more interest upon my old camp ground on the Piedras Pintos, the first I made after leaving Fort Clark three

months before, than any object since. We could easily have
gone on to the fort the same day, but it was necessary to "fix
up;" faces must be shaved, and clean shirts and collars, and
sometimes entire changes were necessary. This was my last
opportunity for a hunt, and without waiting for dinner, I
took my gun and started up the creek. I wandered long through
the dry grass and thickets of shrub-oaks, blasted by prairie
fires; a solemn stillness reigned through all the solitude, and
I was startled by the crackling of the dead twigs beneath my
own feet. I discovered a pile of noble turkeys in the edge of
the thicket close to me, but before I could fire they had disappeared. I could hear them one by one fly across the stream,
which was here widened into a lagoon three miles long. I
went around it, and having crossed the stream, was slowly
making my way through the grass, nearly breast high, watching more carefully for Indians than anything else, when a
prodigious rushing noise, not more than six yards from me,
was so suddenly made as to throw me entirely off from my
propriety, and before I could satisfy myself that I was not a
murdered man, a huge gobbler had taken wing, and was making for a thicket. I raised my piece but it would not go off, and
I found too late that I had pulled the wrong trigger. What
vexation! Why do I write of it, but as a lesson to those who
would aspire to be Nimrods.[3] So I returned to camp after an
afternoon of hard toil, faint with hunger, without having fired
a shot, and had the satisfaction of finding that the Major had
killed a splended turkey without having left the camp, and
with his spectacles on his nose. The next morning we rode
into the Fort and finished our long sojourn in the Indian
country. I shook hands with old Major Simonson, Doctor Norris,
and the other officers, as with old friends, and felt it was a
great relief to be among the abodes of men, although I was

---

[3] Nimrod was the son of Cush, described in Gen. 10:8-10. He was a mighty hunter.

still five days' journey from San Antonio, and two from the nearest settlement. I felt relieved from that incessant watchfulness that becomes a habit in a hostile region. And here I will close my "wanderings."

In these letters I have endeavored to give a truthful impression rather than a captivating one. I have avoided any generalizations based upon limited observation. I have avoided narrating anything of which I have not myself been an observer. I went to Texas to satisfy my curiosity, and to study its resources and natural history, and I am confident that those who have felt interest enough in these letters to read them all, have a truer picture of that country than can be found in any other quarter. Of its political, social, and religious condition, I have not written. For the most part, I have avoided the settlements, and found my companionship in the solitudes of the untrodden wilds, and have never felt alone where nature displays so many charms; to her lovers she needs no artificial coloring. To such every region possesses an interest, which those who worship at a false shrine can never appreciate. If I had been disposed to suppress a part of the truth, and give play to fancy, no country that I have ever visited affords a better field. Nowhere have I seen nature display so much of chastened beauty, or rugged grandeur, as in the regions I have attempted to describe; nowhere have I seen realized, in so high a degree, the charms of the classical *Arcadia* as in the rolling grassy regions of Western Texas. Its landscapes ever varying, yet always beautiful; its sparkling waters bursting at once from their rocky caverns into the glad sunlight; its skies and healthful breezes breathing a perpetual inspiration of strength to the invalid, all invite him and the thousand homeless ones to its bosom. In few countries will one find so much done by nature to prepare the ground for the settler, and so little by art. It is in the raising of stock that the chief wealth of the country will in the future consist.

Cattle require no other attention than is necessary to keep them from straying too far; and marking, to enable the owner to identify them; and no occupation can be more healthful to the tuberculous invalid than the care of them. Mexican herdsmen can be employed at from five to ten dollars per month and rations, and often make better field hands than negroes, and the loss is not so great if they run away, which, from the vicinity of the Mexican frontier, the negroes are prone to do; so that as a general rule few of them are employed there for such purposes. Stock cattle can be bought for seven dollars a head, and any one who is at all acquainted with the business can calculate their rate of increase better than I. It is sufficient to say that those who are in the business are becoming rapidly wealthy. To any one desirous of visiting the country, and spending a few months in investigating the resources of the country, for the purpose of settlement, or pursuit of health, or enjoyment of nature in her "visible forms" and primitive loveliness, I would recommend to leave the steamer at Indianola and take the mail coach to San Antonio. The time occupied is forty-eight hours. At the latter place, one can purchase a pony enough cheaper to pay the fare (fifteen dollars) in the coach, and making that place his head-quarters, he can suit his journeyings to his convenience. A saddle made in San Antonio is the best, and most salable when he has no longer use for it. His travel may be extended alone in perfect safety, South and East, and in small parties, well armed, in any other direction. He should be provided with a good fowling-piece, which, taken all in all, is the best weapon for that country, and the sooner he learns to sleep on the ground with a blanket and his saddle, the better. He will save many a half-dollar otherwise spent for a worse bed, and the invalid who has strength to ride, may do so with perfect impunity, nay, even with benefit. And if he knows how to use his gun he will need but few stores that he cannot carry in his saddle-bags. He will find settlements, if he chooses, sufficiently frequent to meet emergencies, and if, through any mischance, he should find himself "hard up," he will find friends according to his merits, as generous and hospitable as in any part of the world, and more than one can realize who has been dragging out his existence among the cold, calculating conventionalisms of our old towns and settlements. He will learn that happiness does not consist in the amount of luxuries which may be heaped about him, nor in the approbations of the purse-proud and soulless creatures, who know not God except in their prayers, and who see nothing in the face of all His magnificent creations to admire but themselves and the work of their own hands. He will return from his wanderings a healthier, wiser, and a better man.

J.D.B.S.

Bibliography

Primary Sources

Manuscripts

Hampton, Joseph Wade, Papers. Archives, Austin College Library, Sherman, Tex.

O'Connor, Kathryn Stoner. Notes on J. D. B. Stillman's "Wanderings in the Southwest." Supplied to the editor by Margaret Stoner McLean of Arlington, Tex.

"Population Schedule of the Eighth Census of the United States, 1860." National Archives. Microfilm copy, Fort Worth Public Library.

Printed Government Documents

Emory, William H. *Report on the United States and Mexican Boundary Survey,* 34th Cong., 1st Sess., H. E. D. 135. Two vols. Washington: A. O. P. Nicholson, 1857, 1859.

Hamersly, Thomas H. S., comp. *Complete Regular Army Register of the United States: For One Hundred Years, (1779-1879).* Washington: T. H. S. Hamersly, 1880.

Heitman, Francis B., comp. *Historical Register and Dictionary of the United States Army.* Washington: Govt. Printing Office, 1903.

Official Army Register of 1855. Washington: Adj. Gen. Office, 1855.

Newspapers

Alamo Star (San Antonio), 1854.

The Crayon (New York), 1855.

Daily Alta California (San Francisco), 1888.

The Galveston Weekly News, 1855.

Neu-Braunfelser Zeitung, 1855.

San Antonio Herald, 1855.

San Antonio Ledger, 1855.

San Antonio Texan, 1855.

San Antonio Zeitung, 1853, 1855.

The Texas Republican (Marshall), 1853-1854.

Texas State Gazette (Austin), 1855.

The Texas State Times (Austin), 1855.

Western Texan (San Antonio), 1851.

Books

Audubon, John James. *The Birds of America.* Edinburgh and London: J. J. Audubon, 1827-1838.

——————. *The Birds of America: From Drawings Made in the United States and Their Territories.* Seven vols. N. Y. and Philadelphia: J. J. Audubon and J. B. Chevalier, 1840-1844.

Bartlett, John Russell. *Personal Narrative of Explorations and Incidents in Texas, New Mexico, California, Sonora and Chihuahua, Connected with the United States and Mexican Boundary Commission, During the Years 1850, '51, '52 and '53.* Two vols. N. Y: D. Appleton & Co., 1854.

Carpenter, V. K., ed. *The State of Texas, Federal Population Schedules: Seventh Census of the United States, 1850.* Five vols. Huntsville, Ark: Century Enterprises, 1969.

Cassin, John. *Illustrations of the Birds of California, Texas, Oregon, British and Russian America.* Philadelphia: J. B. Lippincott & Co., 1856.

DeVoto, Bernard, ed. *The Journals of Lewis and Clark.* Boston: Houghton Mifflin Co., 1953.

Ford, John S. *Rip Ford's Texas.* Ed. by Stephen B. Oates. Austin: Univ. of Tex. Press, 1963.

Geue, Ethel Hander, ed. *New Homes in a New Land: German Immigration to Texas, 1847-1861.* Waco: Texian Press, 1970.

——————— and Chester W. Geue, comps. and eds. *A New Land Beckoned: German Immigration to Texas, 1844-1847.* Waco: Texian Press, 1966.

Gray, A. B. *Survey of a Route for the Southern Pacific R.R., on the 32nd Parallel by A. B. Gray, for the Texas Western R.R. Company.* Cincinnati: Wrightson & Co.'s ("Railroad Record.") Print, 1856. Reprinted in L. R. Bailey, ed. *The A. B. Gray Report: Survey of a Route on the 32nd Parallel for the Texas Western Railroad, 1854, and Including the Reminiscences of Peter R. Brady Who Accompanied the Expedition.* Los Angeles: Westernlore Press, 1963.

Hawke, David Freeman, ed. *The Cotton Kingdom: A Selection.* Indianapolis: Bobbs-Merrill Co., 1971.

McLaughlin, Charles Capen, and Charles E. Beveridge, eds. *The Papers of Frederick Law Olmsted: The Formative Years, 1822 to 1852.* Three vols. Baltimore: Johns Hopkins Univ. Press, 1977-1983.

New Map of the State of Texas as It Is in 1875. N. Y: G. W. and C. B. Colton, 1847.

Olmsted, Frederick Law. *A Journey Through Texas; or, A Saddle-Trip on the Southwestern Frontier: With a Statistical Appendix.* N. Y: Dix, Edwards & Co., 1857.

————. *A Journey to the Seaboard Slave States, with Remarks on Their Economy.* N. Y: Dix and Edwards, 1856.

Roemer, Ferdinand. *Texas With Particular Reference to German Immigration and the Physical Appearance of the Country.* Trans. by Oswald Mueller. San Antonio: Standard Printing Co., 1935.

Stillman, Jacob D. B. *An 1850 Voyage: San Francisco to Baltimore by Sea and by Land.* Intro. by John Barr Tompkins. Palo Alto: Lewis Osborne, 1967.

————. *Around the Horne to California in 1849.* Foreword by Kenneth M. Johnson. Palo Alto: Lewis Osborne, 1967.

————. *Catalogue of Books to be Sold at Auction on Friday, September 24, 1880, Being the Medical and Miscellaneous Library of Dr. J. D. B. Stillman, Comprising Many Rare and Valuable English Books* . . . [San Francisco]: Alta California Printing House, [1880].

————. *The Gold Rush Letters of J. D. B. Stillman.* Intro. by Kenneth Johnson. Palo Alto: Lewis Osborne, 1967.

————. *The Horse in Motion as Shown by Instantaneous Photography with a Study on Animal Mechanics. Founded on Anatomy and the Revelations of the Camera, in Which is Demonstrated the Theory of Quadrupedal Locomotion.* Boston: J. R. Osgood and Co., 1882.

————. *Seeking the Golden Fleece; a Record of Pioneer Life in California: To Which is Annexed Footprints of Early Navigators, Other Than Spanish, in California; With an Account of the Voyage of the Schooner Dolphin.* San Francisco and N.Y: A. Roman & Co., 1877.

Winfrey, Dorman H., and James M. Day, eds. *Indian Papers of Texas and the Southwest, 1825-1916.* Five vols. Austin: Pemberton Press, 1966.

Articles

Allingham, William. "The Fairies," *Oxford Dictionary of Quotations.* 2nd ed. London: Oxford Univ. Press, 1966.

Crimmins, M. L., ed. "W. G. Freeman's Report on the Eighth Military Department," *Southwestern Hist. Quar.,* LIII (July, 1949).

Whiting, William Henry Chase. "Journal of William Henry Chase Whiting, 1849," in Ralph P. Bieber, ed. *Exploring Southwestern Trails, 1846-1854*. Glendale: Arthur H. Clark Co., 1938.

Secondary Sources

Books

Alexander, Drury Blakely. *Texas Homes of the Nineteenth Century*. Austin: Univ. of Tex. Press, 1966.

Barlow, Elizabeth, and William Alex. *Frederick Law Olmsted's New York*. N. Y: Praeger Publishers, 1972.

Bender, Averam B. *The March of Empire: Frontier Defense in the Southwest, 1848-1860*. Lawrence: Univ. of Kan. Press, 1952.

Biesele, Rudolph Leopold. *The History of the German Settlements in Texas, 1831-1861*. Austin: Press of Von Boeckmann-Jones Co., 1930.

Botting, Douglas. *Humboldt and the Cosmos*. N. Y: Harper & Row Publishers, 1973.

Coulter, Ellis M. *Travels in the Confederate States, a Bibliography*. Norman: Univ. of Okla. Press, 1948.

Day, James M., comp. *Maps of Texas, 1527-1900*. Austin: Pemberton Press, 1964.

Fabos, Julius Gy., Gordon T. Milde, and V. Michael Weinmayr. *Frederick Law Olmsted, Sr.: Founder of Landscape Architecture in America*. Amherst: Univ. of Mass. Press, 1968.

Fein, Albert. *Frederick Law Olmsted and the American Environmental Tradition*. N. Y: George Braziller, Inc., 1972.

Ferguson, Walter Keene. *Geology and Politics in Frontier Texas, 1845-1909*. Austin: Univ. of Tex. Press, 1969.

Friend, Llerena B. *Sam Houston: The Great Designer*. Austin: Univ. of Tex. Press, 1954.

Goetzmann, William H. *Army Exploration in the American West, 1803-1863*. New Haven: Yale Univ. Press, 1959.

Goodman, David Michael. *A Western Panorama, 1849-1875: The Travels, Writings and Influence of J. Ross Browne*. Glendale: Arthur H. Clark Co., 1966.

Greer, James K. *Colonel Jack Hays: Texas Frontier Leader and California Builder*. N. Y: E. P. Dutton, 1952.

Haas, Oscar. *History of New Braunfels and Comal County, Texas, 1844-1846*. Austin: privately printed, 1968.

Haas, Robert Bartlett. *Eadweard Muybridge: The Stanford Years, 1872-1882*. Palo Alto, Calif: Stanford Univ. Art Museum, 1972.

—————. *Muybridge: Man in Motion*. Berkeley: Univ. of California Press, 1976.

Hogan, William Ransom. *The Texas Republic: A Social and Economic History*. Austin: Univ. of Tex. Press, 1969 reprint.

Jenkins, John H. *Basic Texas Books: An Annotated Bibliography of Selected Works for a Research Library*. Austin: Jenkins Publishing Co., 1983.

Johnson's New Map of The State of Texas. N. Y: Johnson and Browning, 1861.

Lathrop, Barnes F. *Migration Into East Texas, 1835-1860: A Study from the United States Census*. Austin: Texas State Hist. Assn., 1949.

Malsch, Brownson. *Indianola: The Mother of Western Texas*. Austin: Shoal Creek Publishers, Inc., 1977.

Meinig, D. W. *Imperial Texas: An Interpretive Essay in Cultural Geography*. Austin: Univ. of Tex. Press, 1969.

Nackman, Mark E. *A Nation Within a Nation: The Rise of Texas Nationalism*. Port Washington, N. Y: Kennikat Press, 1975.

Newcomb, W. W., Jr. *The Rock Art of Texas Indians*. Austin: Univ. of Tex. Press, 1967.

Novak, Barbara. *Nature and Culture: American Landscape and Painting, 1825-1875*. N. Y: Oxford Univ. Press, 1980.

Olmsted, Frederick Law, Jr., and Theodora Kimball, eds. *Frederick Law Olmstead, Landscape Architect, 1822-1903*. N. Y: G. P. Putnam's, 1922 and 1928.

Raines, C. W. *A Bibliography of Texas: Being a Descriptive List of Books, Pamphlets, and Documents Relating to Texas in Print and Manuscript Since 1536 . . .* Austin: Gammel Book Co., 1896.

Ramsdell, Charles. *San Antonio: A Historical and Pictorial Guide*. 2nd rev. ed. by Carmen Perry with Charles J. Long. Austin: Univ. of Tex. Press, 1985.

Robertson, Priscilla. *Revolutions of 1848, a Social History*. N. Y: Harper Torchbook, 1960.

Rose, Victor M. *A Republication of the Book Most Often Known as Victor Rose's History of Victoria: Some Historical Facts in Regard to the Settlement of Victoria, Texas*. Ed by J. W. Petty, Jr., and Kate Stoner O'Connor. Victoria, Tex: Book Mart, 1961.

Sibley, Marilyn McAdams. *Travelers in Texas, 1761-1860*. Austin: Univ. of Tex. Press, 1967.

Sowell, A. J. *Early Settlers and Indian Fighters of Southwest Texas.* Austin: Ben C. Jones & Co., Printers, 1900.

Steinfeldt, Cecelia. *Texas Folk Art: One Hundred Fifty Years of the Southwestern Tradition.* Austin: Texas Monthly Press, 1981.

Texas Almanac and State Industrial Guide, 1970-1971. Dallas: A. H. Belo Corp., 1969.

Thonhoff, Robert H. *San Antonio Stage Lines, 1847-1881.* El Paso: Texas Western Press, Univ. of Tex. at El Paso, Southwestern Studies Monograph No. 29, 1971.

Walker, Henry Pickering. *The Wagonmasters: High Plains Freighting from the Earliest Days of the Santa Fé Trail to 1880.* Norman: Univ. of Okla. Press, 1966.

Weaver, Bobby D. *Castro's Colony: Empresario Development in Texas, 1842-1865.* College Station: Tex. A&M Univ. Press, 1985.

Webb, Walter Prescott, H. Bailey Carroll, and Eldon S. Branda, eds. *The Handbook of Texas.* Three vols. Austin: Tex. State Hist. Assn., 1952, 1976.

Yoakum, Henderson. *History of Texas, From Its First Settlement in 1685 to Its Annexation to the United States in 1846.* Two vols. N. Y: Redfield, 1855.

Articles

Lyman, George D. "The Scalpel Under Three Flags in California," *Calif. Hist. Soc. Quar.,* IV (June 1925).

Smith, Ralph A. "The Comanche Bridge Between Oklahoma and Mexico, 1843-1844," *Chronicles of Oklahoma,* XXXIX (Spring 1961).

Tyler, Ronnie C. "Fugitive Slaves in Mexico," *Jour. of Negro Hist.,* LVII (January 1972).

————. "The Callahan Expedition of 1855: Indians or Negroes?" *Southwestern Hist. Quar.,* LXX (Apr. 1967).

Unpublished Theses

Warburton, Sister Margaret Rose. "A History of the O'Connor Ranch, 1834-1939." Unpublished M. A. Thesis, Catholic Univ. of Amer., Washington, D.C.

Index

Alamo, battle of: 88

Alamo: see San Antonio de Valero

Alsatians, settle in Castroville: 54

Amon Carter Museum, Fort Worth, Tx: 22

Anaqua, Tx: 17, 35

Andy, a driver: 126, 127

Angler, a correspondent of *The Crayon*: 105

animals in Tx: red deer, 30; horses, wild, 37; pigs, 39, 46; grey wolf, 40; turtles, 40, 56; panther, 46; rabbit, 57, 101, 142; squirrel, 57, 133; bats, 88; rat, 100; jaguar, 102, 118; puma, 118; tiger cat, 118; deer, 118, 128, 142; prairie dog, 130, 135; antelopes, 135, 142; horned frog, 141; hare, 142; bears, 142; marmot, 142; wolf, 142; lizards, 173; hogs, 174

Antonio, Stillman's traveling companion: 91, 93, 95, 108, 109, 110, 111

Apache Indians: 137

Aranama College, in Goliad, Tx: 41n

Audubon, John James: 29n

Barker, Mr: 51

Bartlett, John Russell: 53n

Beardall, Pvt. James: 146, 149, 156, 160, 164, 165, 166

Beaver Lake: 129

Behr, Judge Otto (Ottmar) von: accompanies Stillman to the *sängerfest*, 59, 59n, 64, 73

Bellevue Hospital, NYC, Stillman physician at: 15

Berlandier, Jean Louis: 29n

birds in Tx: 29n; meadow-lark, 26; doves, 26, 40; blackbirds, 29, 37, 122; lark, 30; sparrow, 30; turtle dove, 30; nighthawk, 30, 34; blue heron, 32; cardinal grosbeak, 36; white crane, 37; plover, 38; turkeys, 39, 101, 113, 118, 129, 134, 174, 176; ducks, 40, 49, 134; Mergansers, 49; hawks, 51, 141; mocking-bird, 56, 175; quail, 57, 101, 112, 118, 124, 141; chuck-wills-widow, 95; whip-poor-will, 96; snake bird, 105; *Ortyx texana*, 123, kingfisher, 141; blue winged teal, 142; road-runner, 156; cardinal, 175

Black Creek: 96

Black Mr: 118, 118n

blacks: 39

Blair, William C., founder of Aranama College and Paine Female Institute: 41n

Boundary Survey Commission: 120

Buquor, P. L: 52, 52n

Callahan, James H: 100n

Camp Lancaster, Tx: 14, 18; Stillman at, 148, 170, 173

Cape Horn: 15

Carl, Prince, of Solms-Braunfels: 16

Carlshafen, Tx: 16

Carpenter, Capt. Stephen D: 142, 143n, 144, 155, 156, 157, 158, 159, 160, 163, 164, 165, 166, 167, 169, 170; dogs belonging to, 144

Castro, Henri: 55n; *Le Texas in 1845: Castroville Colonie Francaise* (Anvers, 1845), 61

Castroville, Tx: 14; Stillman in, 54, 55, 57, 93, 115; view of, 61; Alsatians settle in, 54

Census: *1848*, 14; *1850*, 14; *1860*, 14

Chaean Creek: 95

Typography: Linotype Granjon and
handset Deepdene, provided by
the Sagebrush Press, Morongo Valley, Calif.

Produced under the Direction of: Robert A. Clark

Copies Printed: 750